Story : Jean-Michel Dupont ✳ Art : Mezzo
Graphic design : Nicole Berthoux ✳ Mezzo
First published in France in 2014 by Glénat
First published in the UK in 2016 by
Faber and Faber Ltd, Bloomsbury House, 74–77 Great Russell Street, London WC1B 3DA
© Glénat, 2014
English translation © Ivanka Hahnenberger, 2016
Printed by Livonia
ISBN 978–0–571–32883–3

1 2 3 4 5 6 7 8 9 10

LOVE IN VAIN

⁓ ROBERT JOHNSON 1911-1938 ⁓

MEZZO - J. M. DUPONT

for Nicole, for Véronique

ff

FABER & FABER

FOREWORD

If you're a lover of the blues, if you have even the slightest interest in the blues, this book is for you.
But you don't need to be a fan of the music to appreciate this portrait of the most famous bluesman of all time.
This book is, quite simply, a masterpiece – the quality of the artwork and the text, the poetry of the writing
and the magnificent illustrations, make each of the book's panels a true work of art.

LAWRENCE COHN
Los Angeles, California
August 2014

Lawrence Cohn is the producer of the Grammy Award-winning album Robert Johnson: The Complete
Recordings. *He is also the editor of the book* Nothing but the Blues.

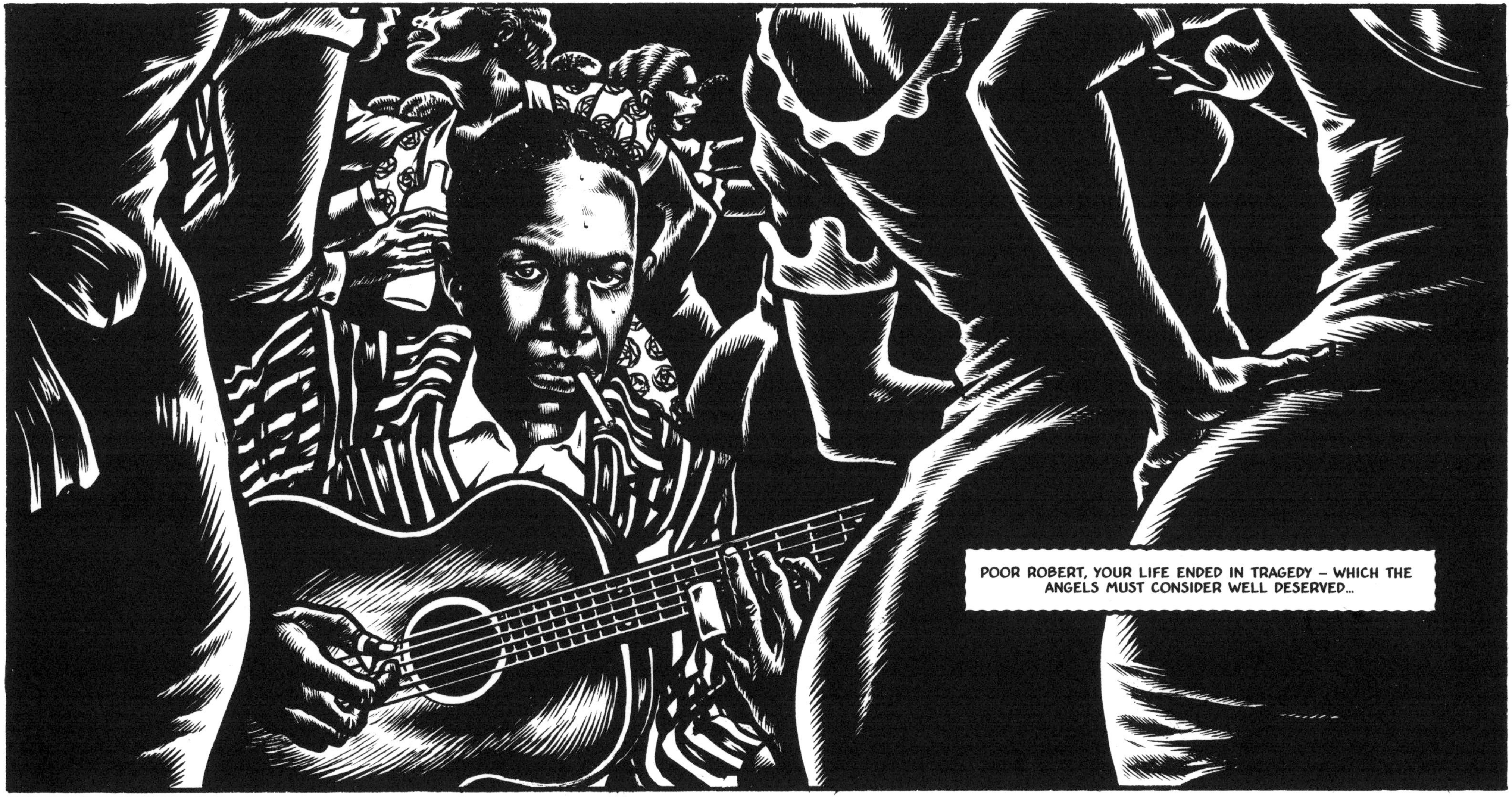
POOR ROBERT, YOUR LIFE ENDED IN TRAGEDY – WHICH THE ANGELS MUST CONSIDER WELL DESERVED...

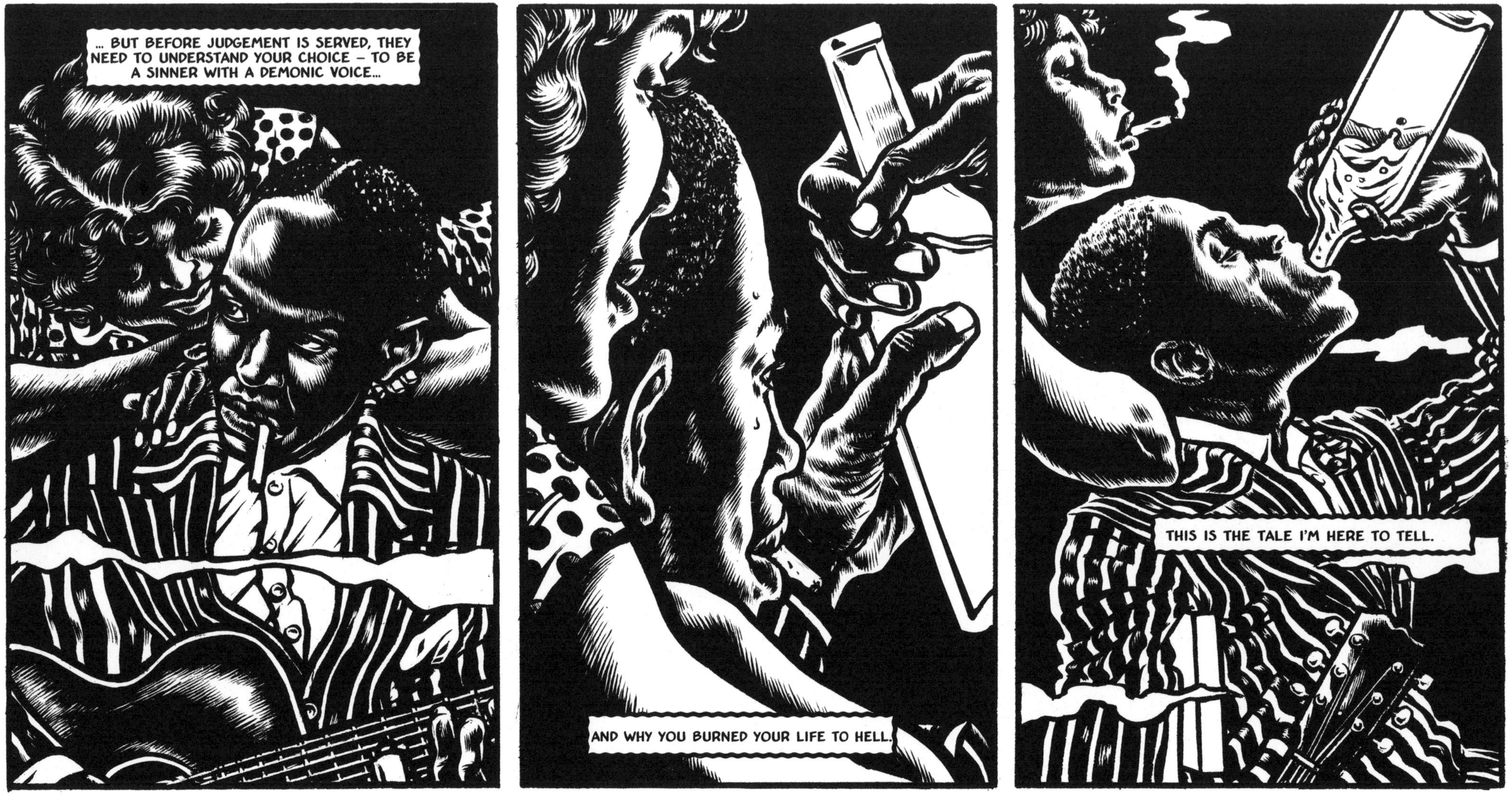
... BUT BEFORE JUDGEMENT IS SERVED, THEY NEED TO UNDERSTAND YOUR CHOICE – TO BE A SINNER WITH A DEMONIC VOICE...
AND WHY YOU BURNED YOUR LIFE TO HELL.
THIS IS THE TALE I'M HERE TO TELL.

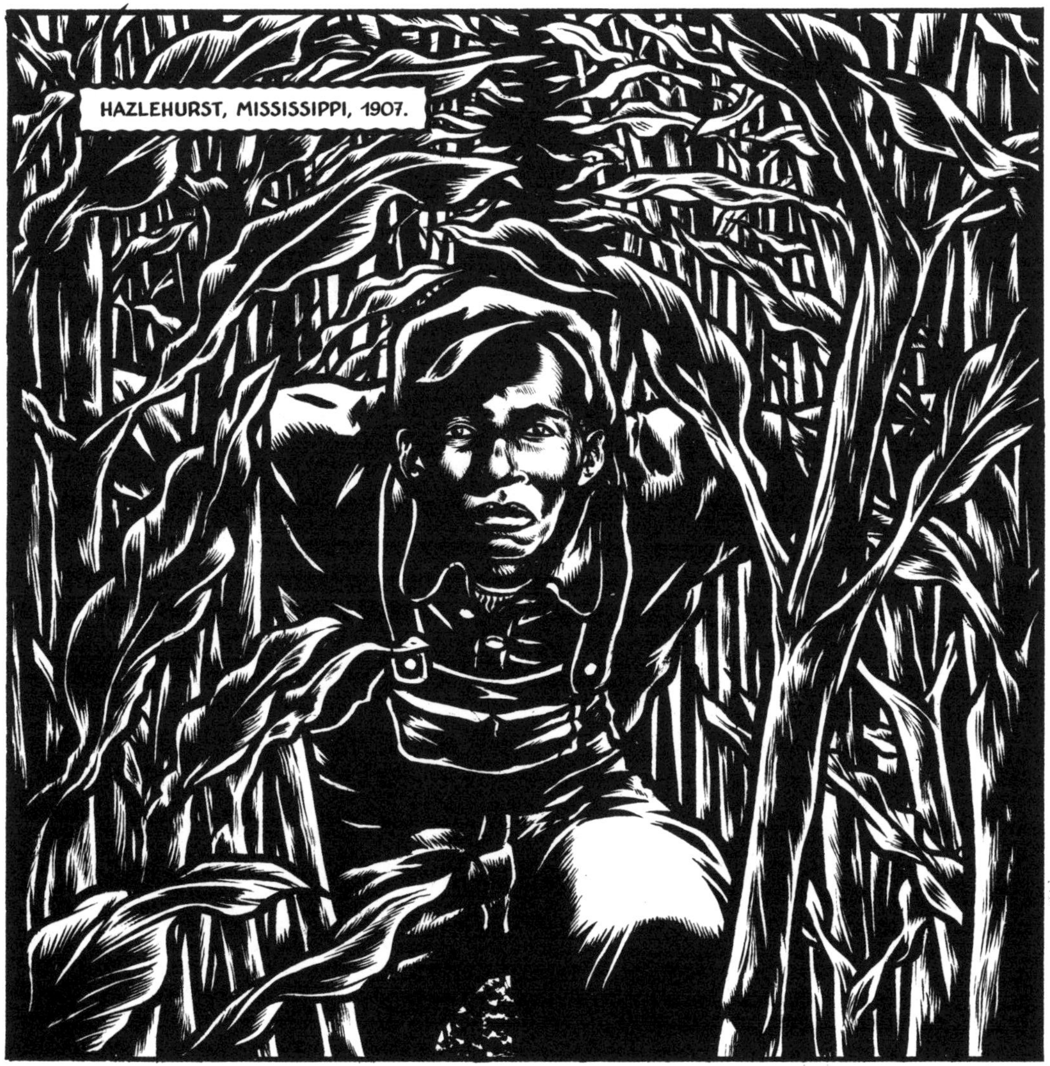
HAZLEHURST, MISSISSIPPI, 1907.

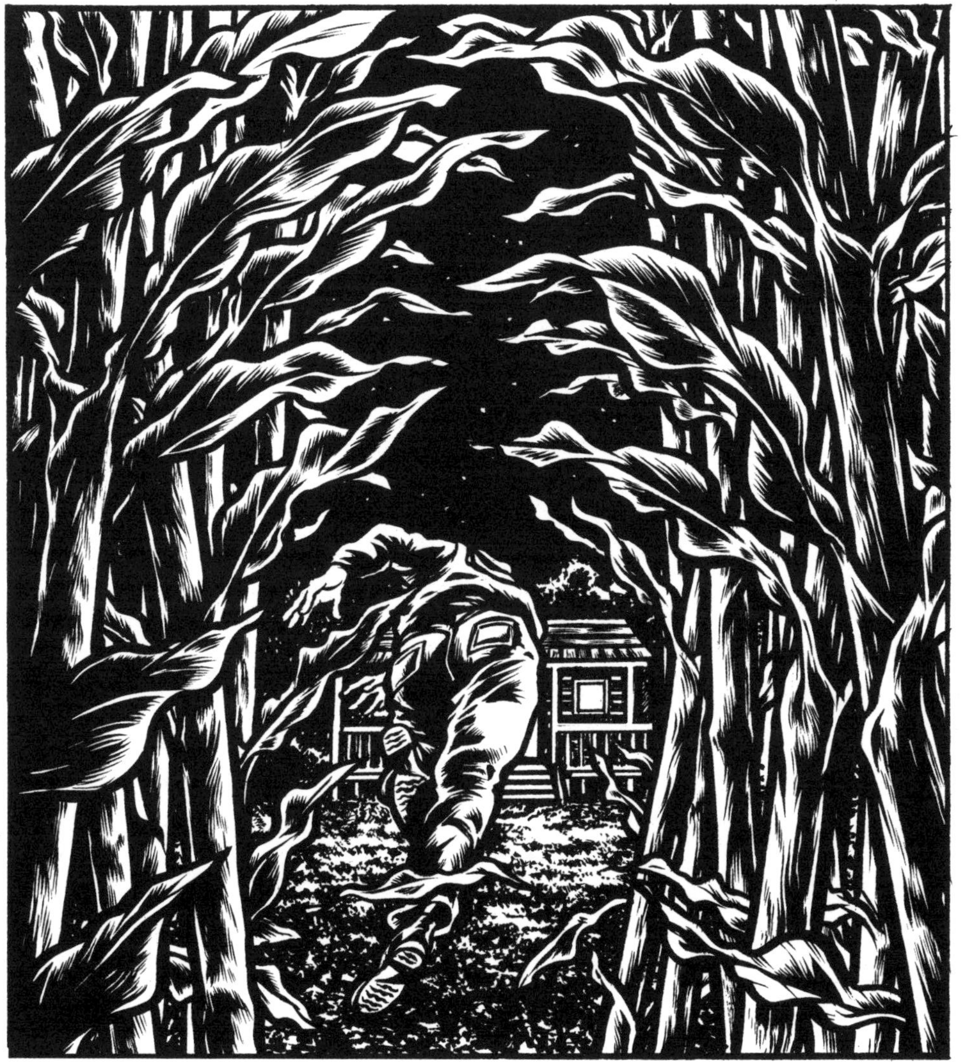

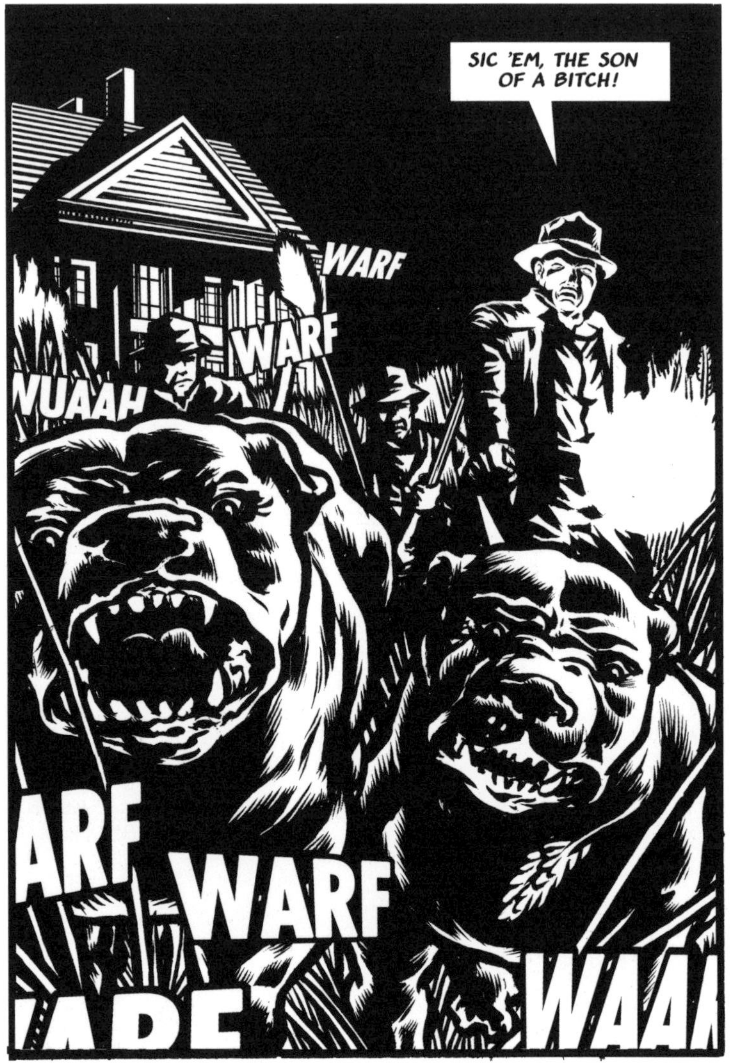
SIC 'EM, THE SON OF A BITCH!
WARF
WARF
WARF

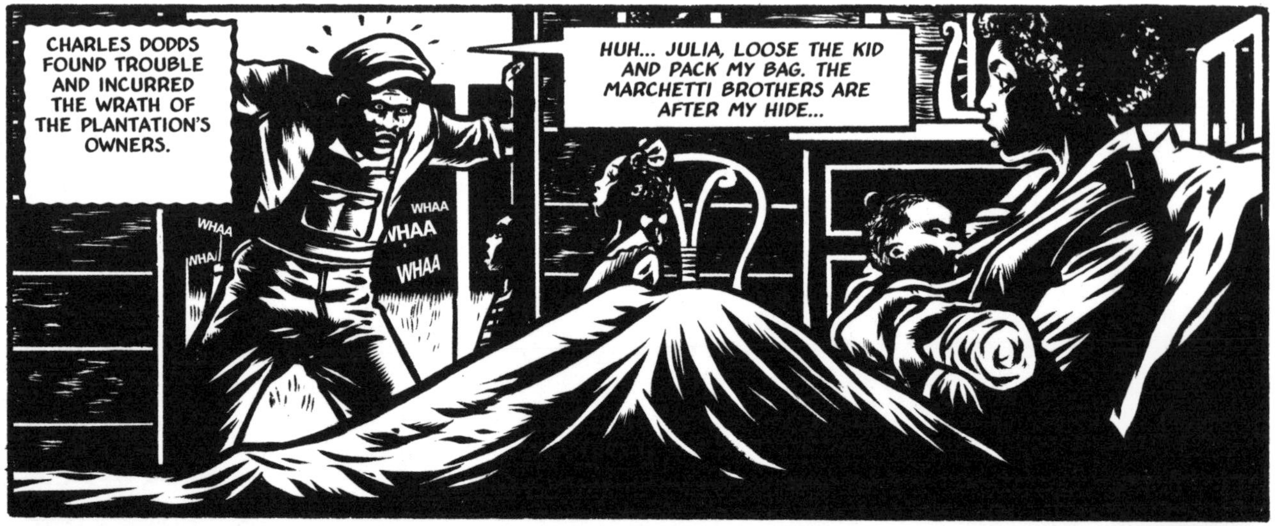
CHARLES DODDS FOUND TROUBLE AND INCURRED THE WRATH OF THE PLANTATION'S OWNERS.
HUH... JULIA, LOOSE THE KID AND PACK MY BAG. THE MARCHETTI BROTHERS ARE AFTER MY HIDE...
WHAA
WHAA
WHAA
WHAA

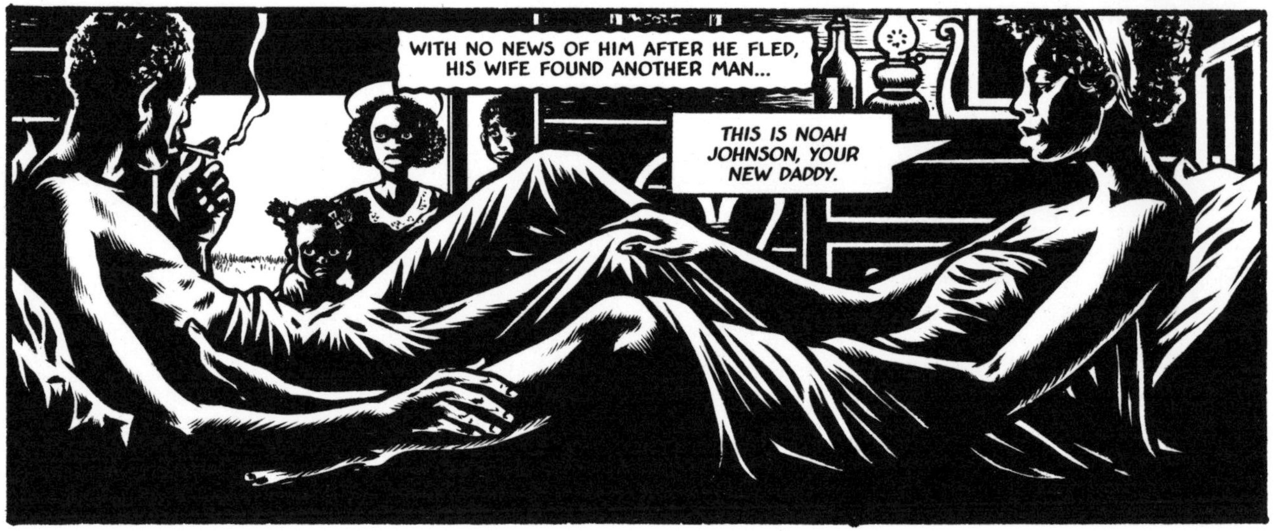
WITH NO NEWS OF HIM AFTER HE FLED, HIS WIFE FOUND ANOTHER MAN...
THIS IS NOAH JOHNSON, YOUR NEW DADDY.

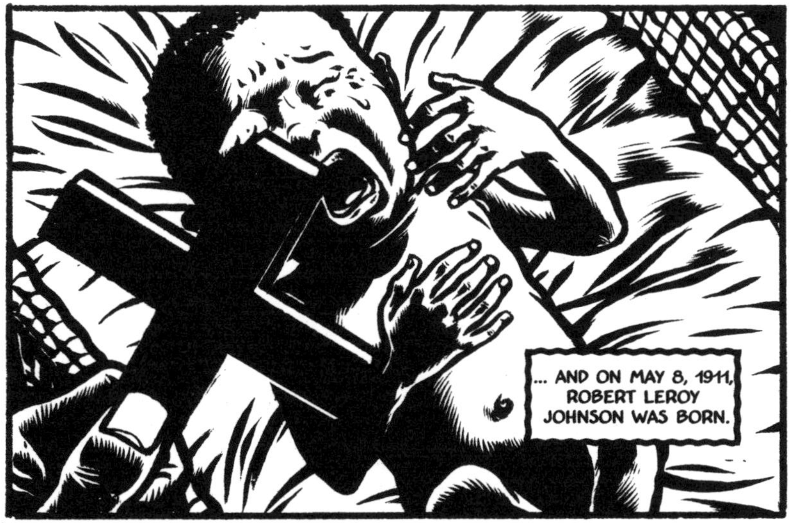
... AND ON MAY 8, 1911, ROBERT LEROY JOHNSON WAS BORN.

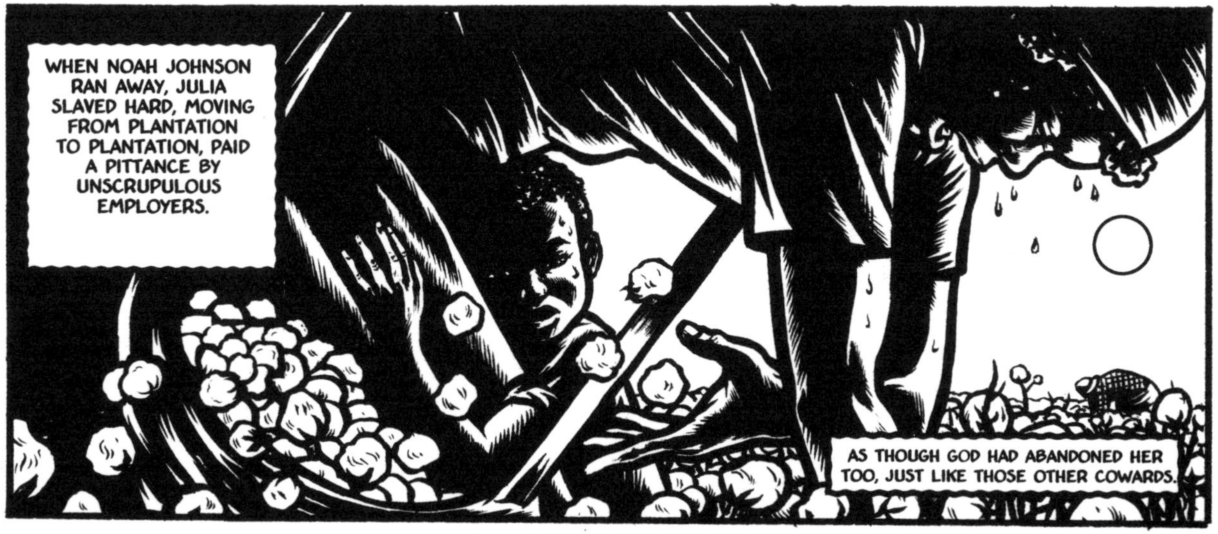
WHEN NOAH JOHNSON RAN AWAY, JULIA SLAVED HARD, MOVING FROM PLANTATION TO PLANTATION, PAID A PITTANCE BY UNSCRUPULOUS EMPLOYERS.
AS THOUGH GOD HAD ABANDONED HER TOO, JUST LIKE THOSE OTHER COWARDS.

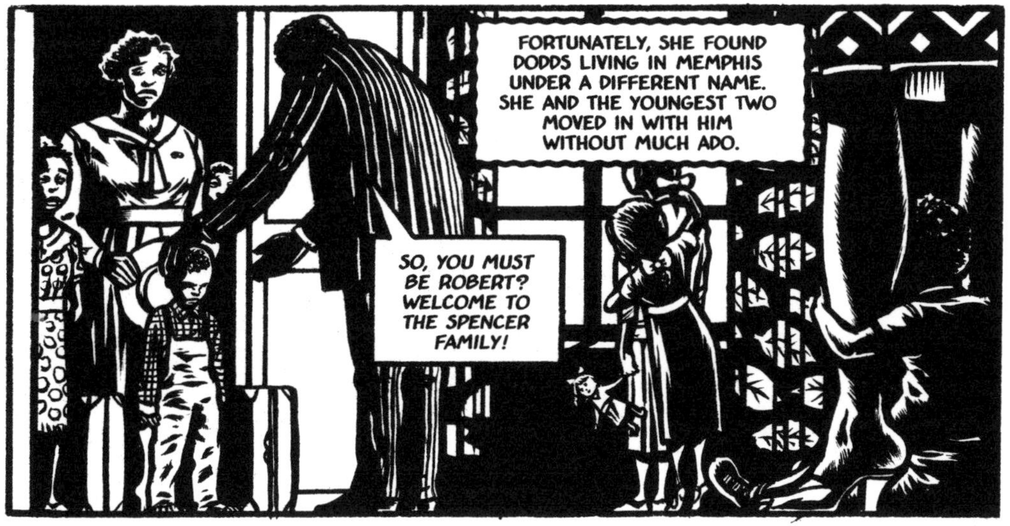
FORTUNATELY, SHE FOUND DODDS LIVING IN MEMPHIS UNDER A DIFFERENT NAME. SHE AND THE YOUNGEST TWO MOVED IN WITH HIM WITHOUT MUCH ADO.
SO, YOU MUST BE ROBERT? WELCOME TO THE SPENCER FAMILY!

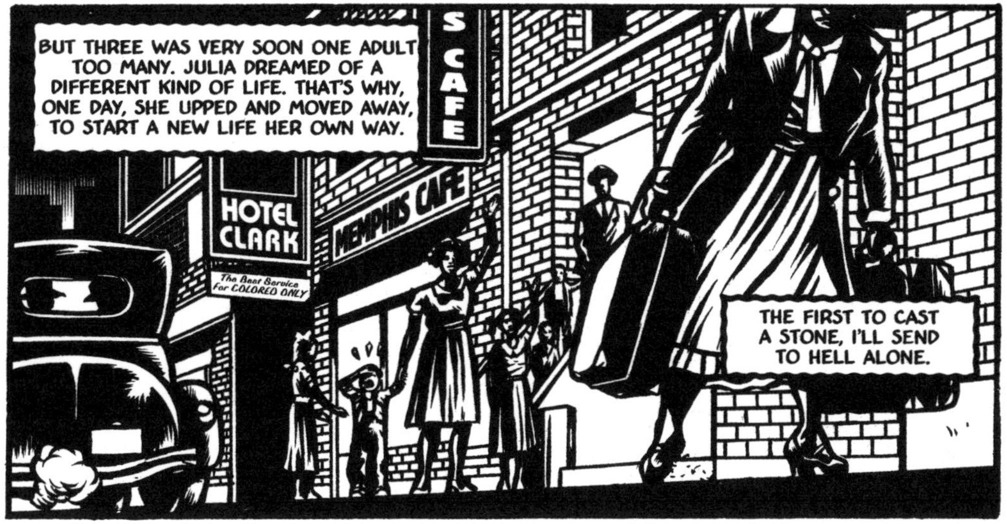
BUT THREE WAS VERY SOON ONE ADULT TOO MANY. JULIA DREAMED OF A DIFFERENT KIND OF LIFE. THAT'S WHY, ONE DAY, SHE UPPED AND MOVED AWAY, TO START A NEW LIFE HER OWN WAY.
S CAFE
HOTEL CLARK
The Best Service For COLORED ONLY
MEMPHIS CAFE
THE FIRST TO CAST A STONE, I'LL SEND TO HELL ALONE.

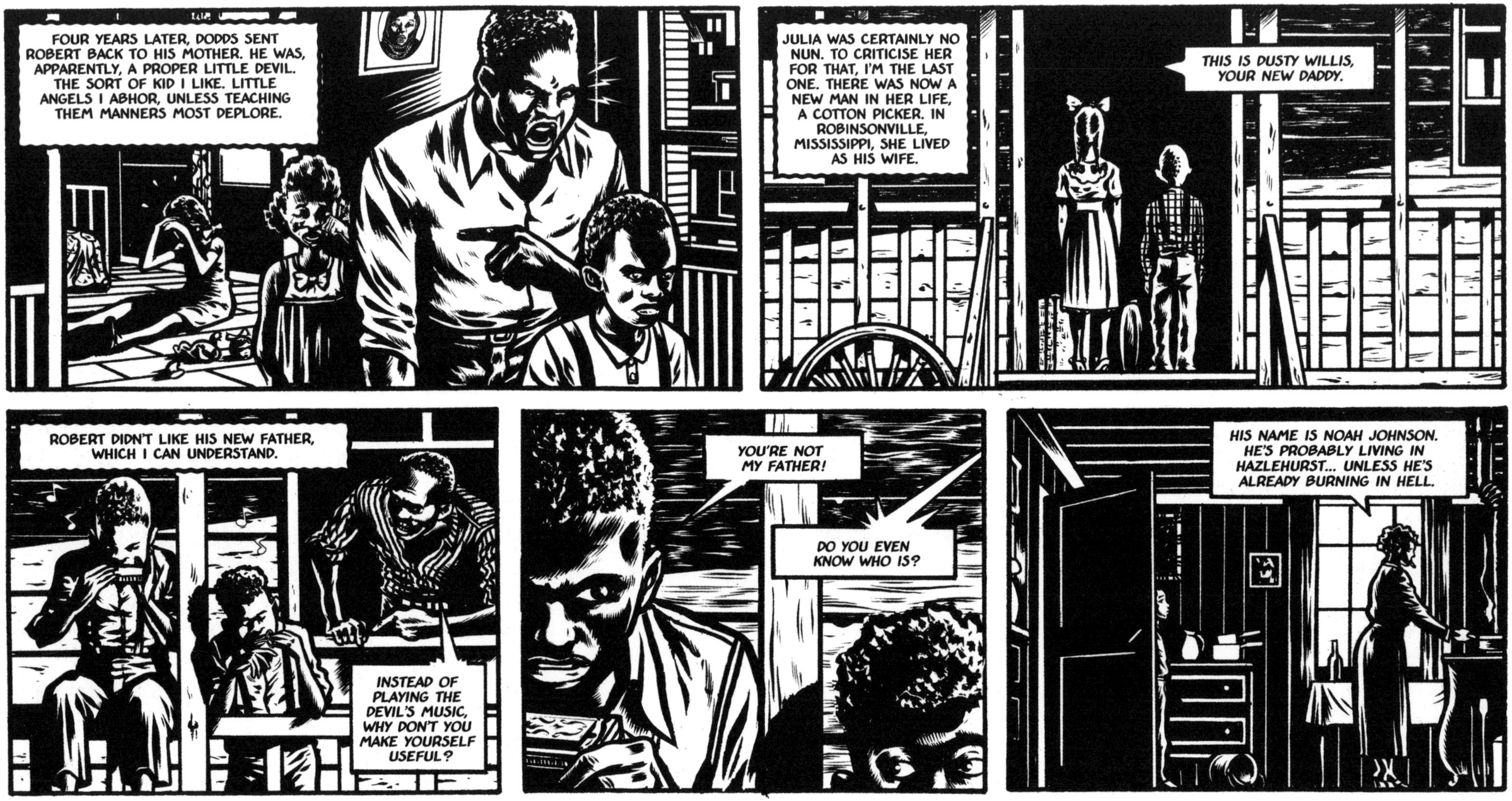
FOUR YEARS LATER, DODDS SENT ROBERT BACK TO HIS MOTHER. HE WAS, APPARENTLY, A PROPER LITTLE DEVIL. THE SORT OF KID I LIKE. LITTLE ANGELS I ABHOR, UNLESS TEACHING THEM MANNERS MOST DEPLORE.
JULIA WAS CERTAINLY NO NUN. TO CRITICISE HER FOR THAT, I'M THE LAST ONE. THERE WAS NOW A NEW MAN IN HER LIFE, A COTTON PICKER. IN ROBINSONVILLE, MISSISSIPPI, SHE LIVED AS HIS WIFE.
THIS IS DUSTY WILLIS, YOUR NEW DADDY.
ROBERT DIDN'T LIKE HIS NEW FATHER, WHICH I CAN UNDERSTAND.
INSTEAD OF PLAYING THE DEVIL'S MUSIC, WHY DON'T YOU MAKE YOURSELF USEFUL?
YOU'RE NOT MY FATHER!
DO YOU EVEN KNOW WHO IS?
HIS NAME IS NOAH JOHNSON. HE'S PROBABLY LIVING IN HAZLEHURST... UNLESS HE'S ALREADY BURNING IN HELL.

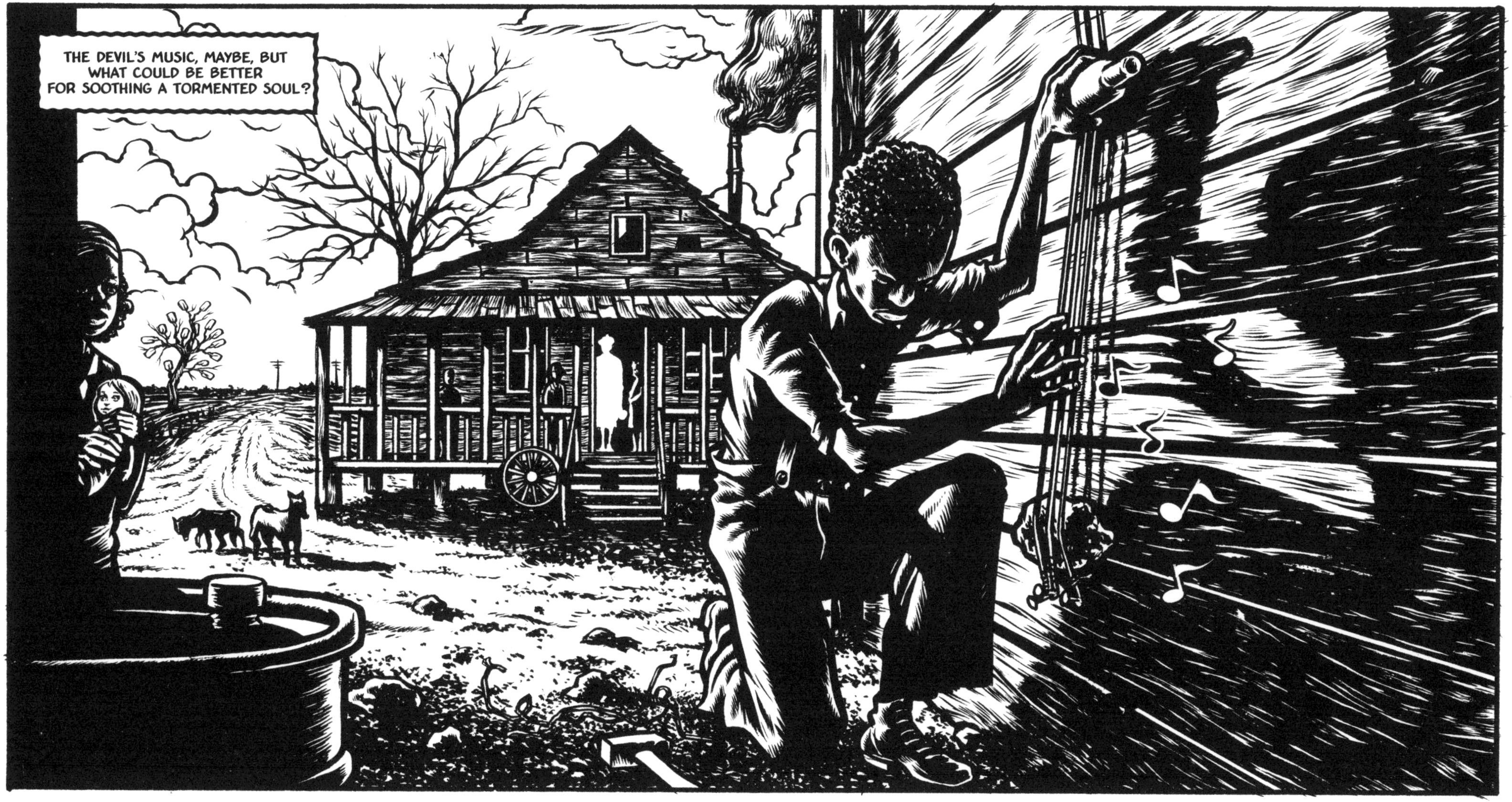
THE DEVIL'S MUSIC, MAYBE, BUT
WHAT COULD BE BETTER
FOR SOOTHING A TORMENTED SOUL?

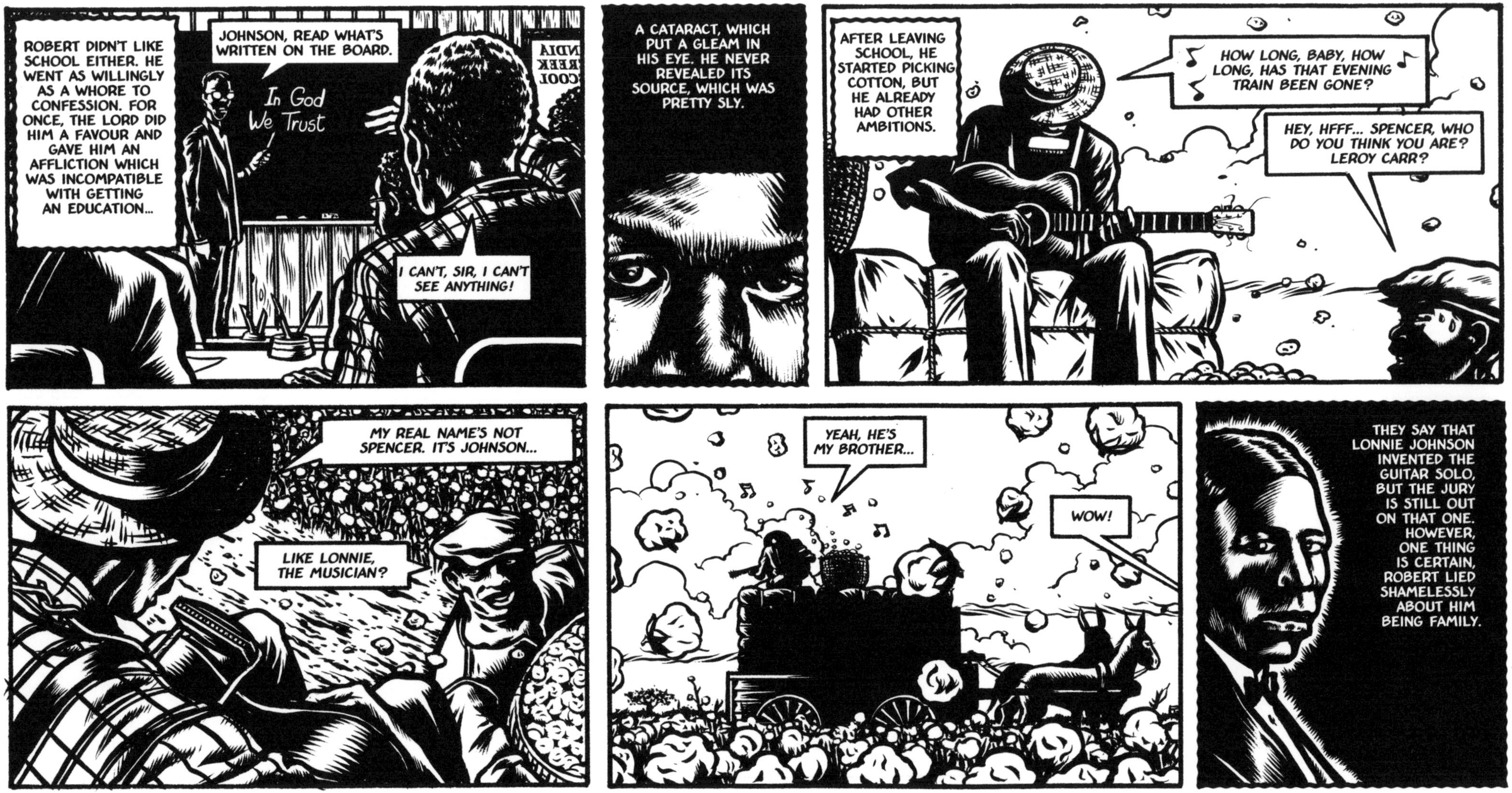
ROBERT DIDN'T LIKE SCHOOL EITHER. HE WENT AS WILLINGLY AS A WHORE TO CONFESSION. FOR ONCE, THE LORD DID HIM A FAVOUR AND GAVE HIM AN AFFLICTION WHICH WAS INCOMPATIBLE WITH GETTING AN EDUCATION...
JOHNSON, READ WHAT'S WRITTEN ON THE BOARD.
In God We Trust
I CAN'T, SIR, I CAN'T SEE ANYTHING!
A CATARACT, WHICH PUT A GLEAM IN HIS EYE. HE NEVER REVEALED ITS SOURCE, WHICH WAS PRETTY SLY.
AFTER LEAVING SCHOOL, HE STARTED PICKING COTTON, BUT HE ALREADY HAD OTHER AMBITIONS.
HOW LONG, BABY, HOW LONG, HAS THAT EVENING TRAIN BEEN GONE?
HEY, HFFF... SPENCER, WHO DO YOU THINK YOU ARE? LEROY CARR?
MY REAL NAME'S NOT SPENCER. IT'S JOHNSON...
LIKE LONNIE, THE MUSICIAN?
YEAH, HE'S MY BROTHER...
WOW!
THEY SAY THAT LONNIE JOHNSON INVENTED THE GUITAR SOLO, BUT THE JURY IS STILL OUT ON THAT ONE. HOWEVER, ONE THING IS CERTAIN, ROBERT LIED SHAMELESSLY ABOUT HIM BEING FAMILY.

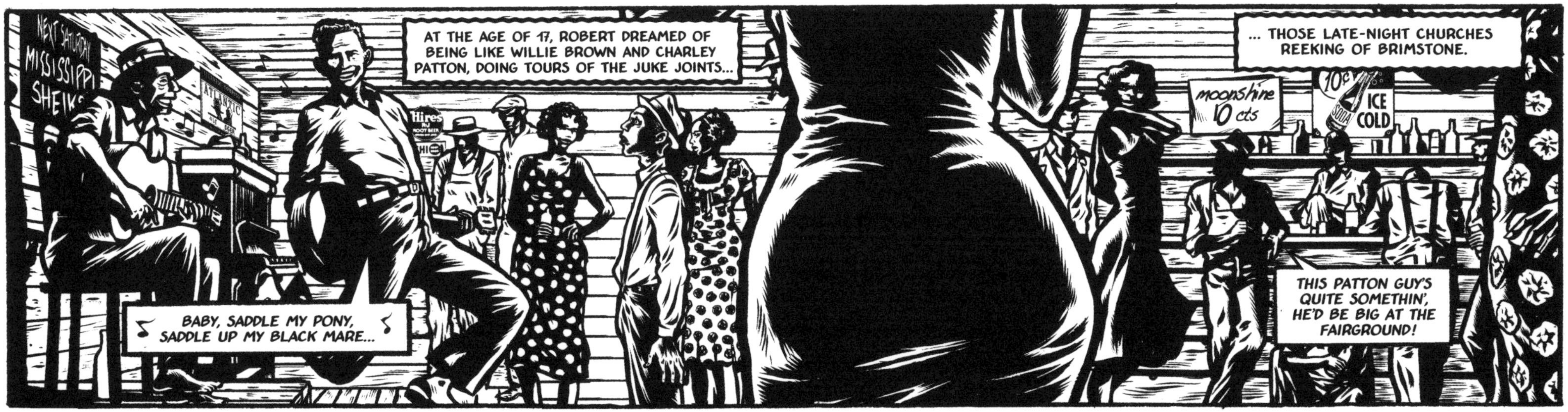
NEXT SATURDAY
MISSISSIPPI SHEIKS
AT THE AGE OF 17, ROBERT DREAMED OF BEING LIKE WILLIE BROWN AND CHARLEY PATTON, DOING TOURS OF THE JUKE JOINTS...
BABY, SADDLE MY PONY, SADDLE UP MY BLACK MARE...
Hires
... THOSE LATE-NIGHT CHURCHES REEKING OF BRIMSTONE.
moonshine 10 cts
ICE COLD
THIS PATTON GUY'S QUITE SOMETHIN', HE'D BE BIG AT THE FAIRGROUND!

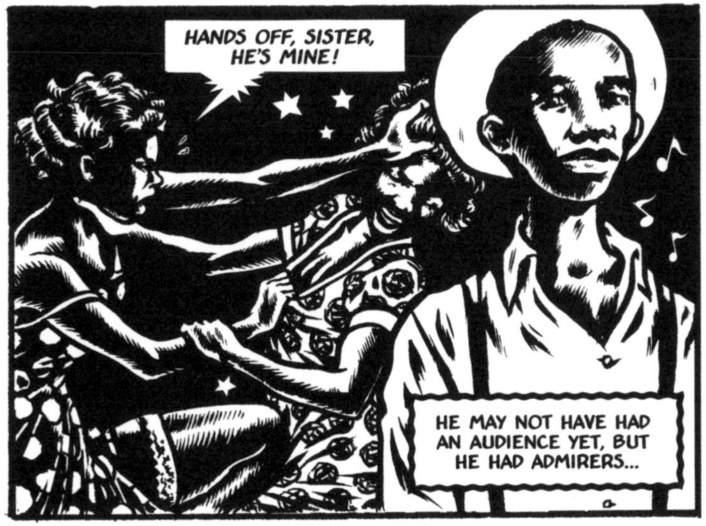
HANDS OFF, SISTER, HE'S MINE!
HE MAY NOT HAVE HAD AN AUDIENCE YET, BUT HE HAD ADMIRERS...

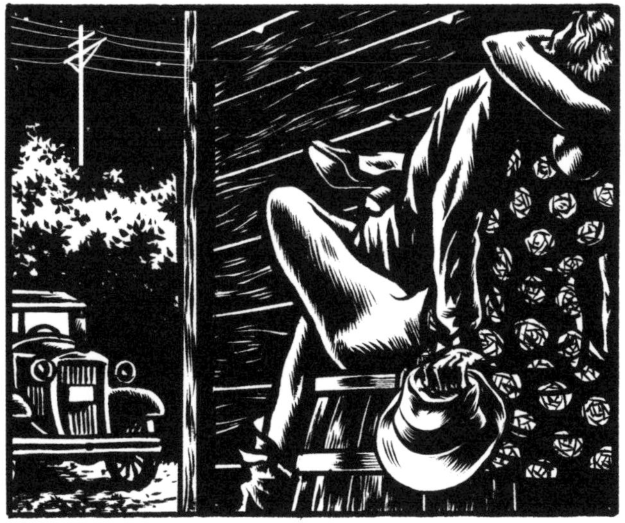

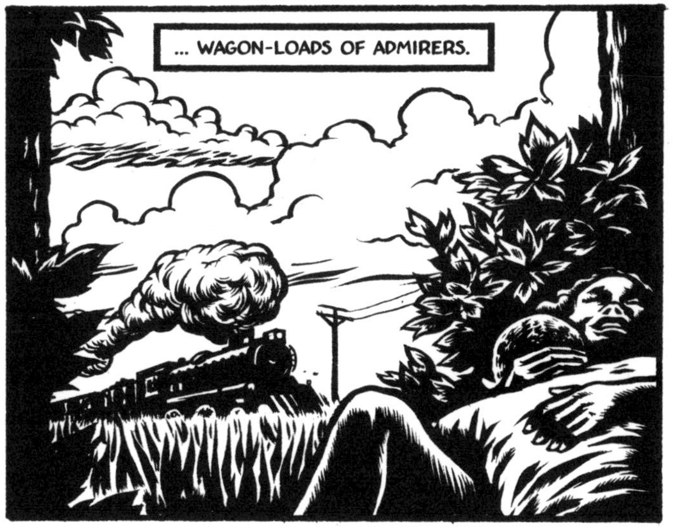
... WAGON-LOADS OF ADMIRERS.

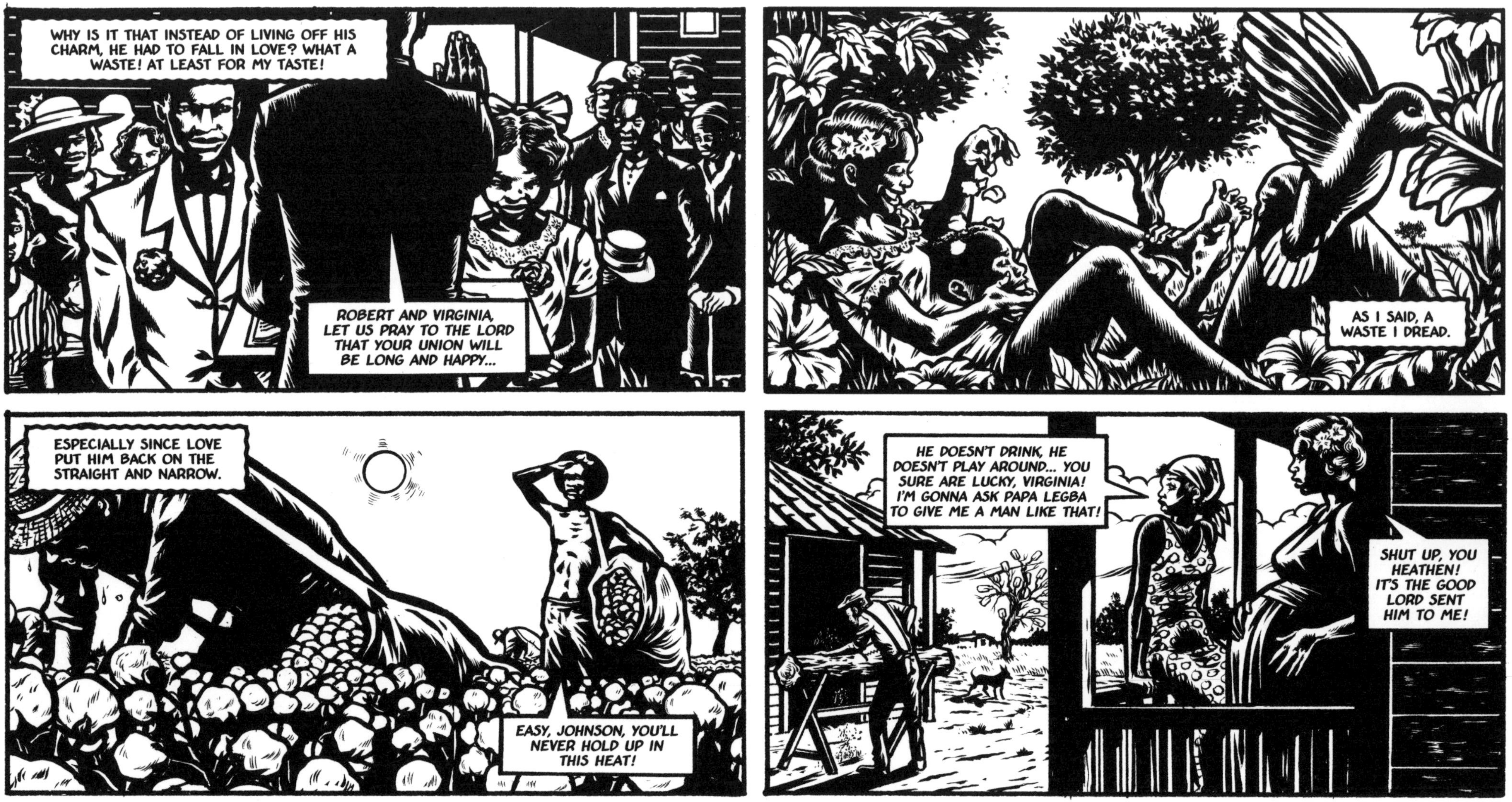
WHY IS IT THAT INSTEAD OF LIVING OFF HIS CHARM, HE HAD TO FALL IN LOVE? WHAT A WASTE! AT LEAST FOR MY TASTE!
ROBERT AND VIRGINIA, LET US PRAY TO THE LORD THAT YOUR UNION WILL BE LONG AND HAPPY...
AS I SAID, A WASTE I DREAD.
ESPECIALLY SINCE LOVE PUT HIM BACK ON THE STRAIGHT AND NARROW.
EASY, JOHNSON, YOU'LL NEVER HOLD UP IN THIS HEAT!
HE DOESN'T DRINK, HE DOESN'T PLAY AROUND... YOU SURE ARE LUCKY, VIRGINIA! I'M GONNA ASK PAPA LEGBA TO GIVE ME A MAN LIKE THAT!
SHUT UP, YOU HEATHEN! IT'S THE GOOD LORD SENT HIM TO ME!

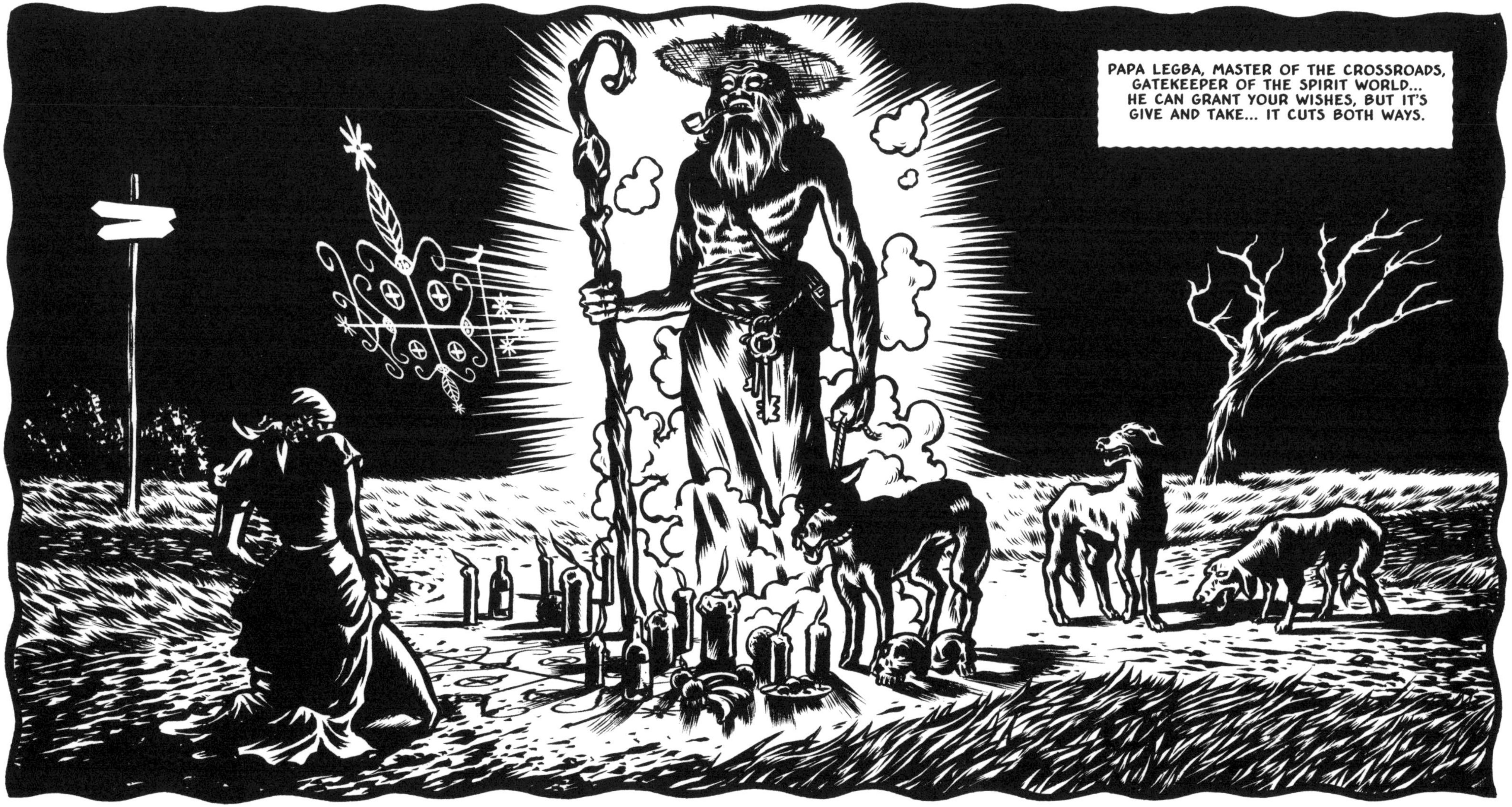
PAPA LEGBA, MASTER OF THE CROSSROADS, GATEKEEPER OF THE SPIRIT WORLD... HE CAN GRANT YOUR WISHES, BUT IT'S GIVE AND TAKE... IT CUTS BOTH WAYS.

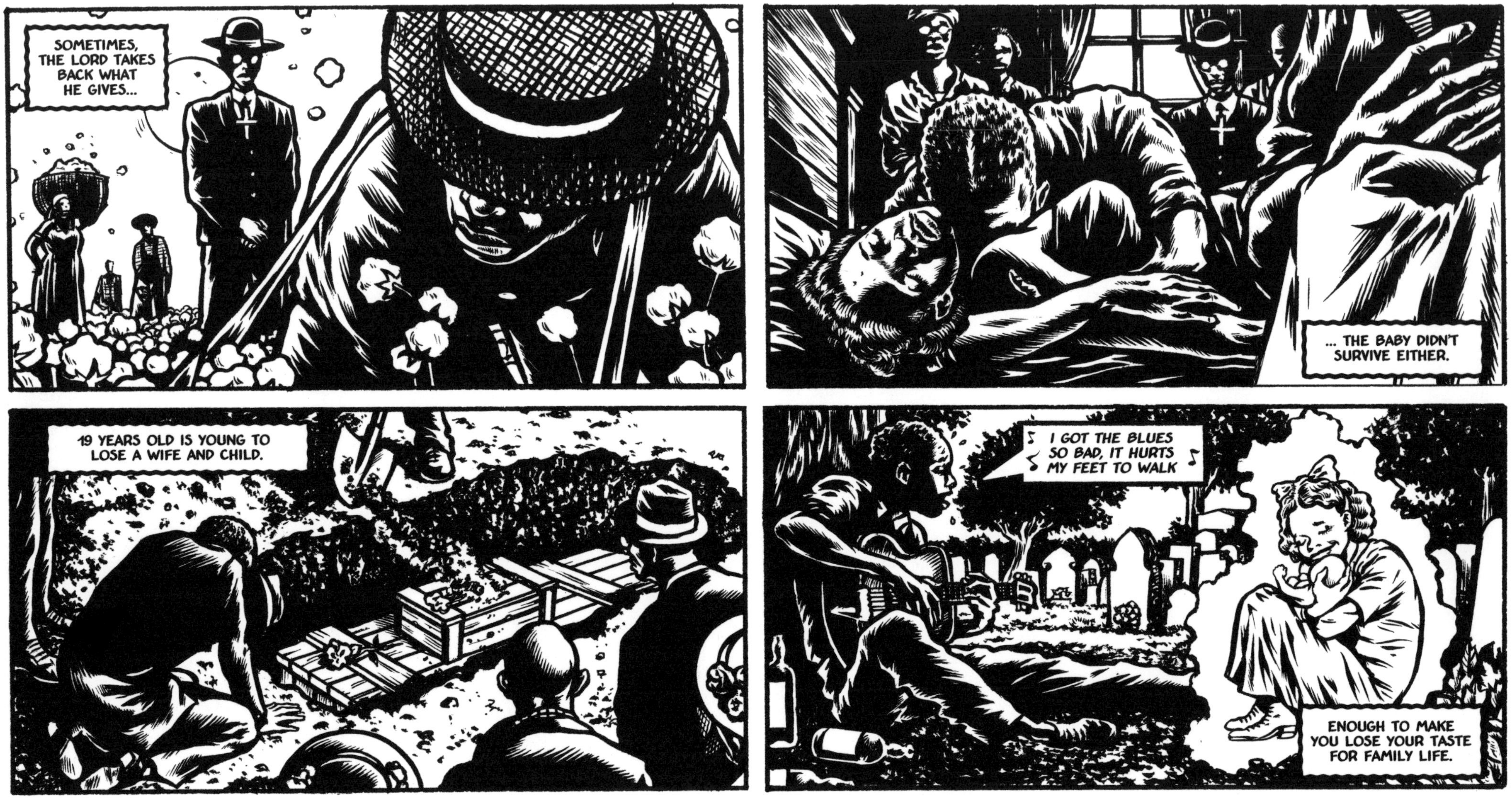
SOMETIMES, THE LORD TAKES BACK WHAT HE GIVES...
... THE BABY DIDN'T SURVIVE EITHER.
19 YEARS OLD IS YOUNG TO LOSE A WIFE AND CHILD.
I GOT THE BLUES SO BAD, IT HURTS MY FEET TO WALK
ENOUGH TO MAKE YOU LOSE YOUR TASTE FOR FAMILY LIFE.

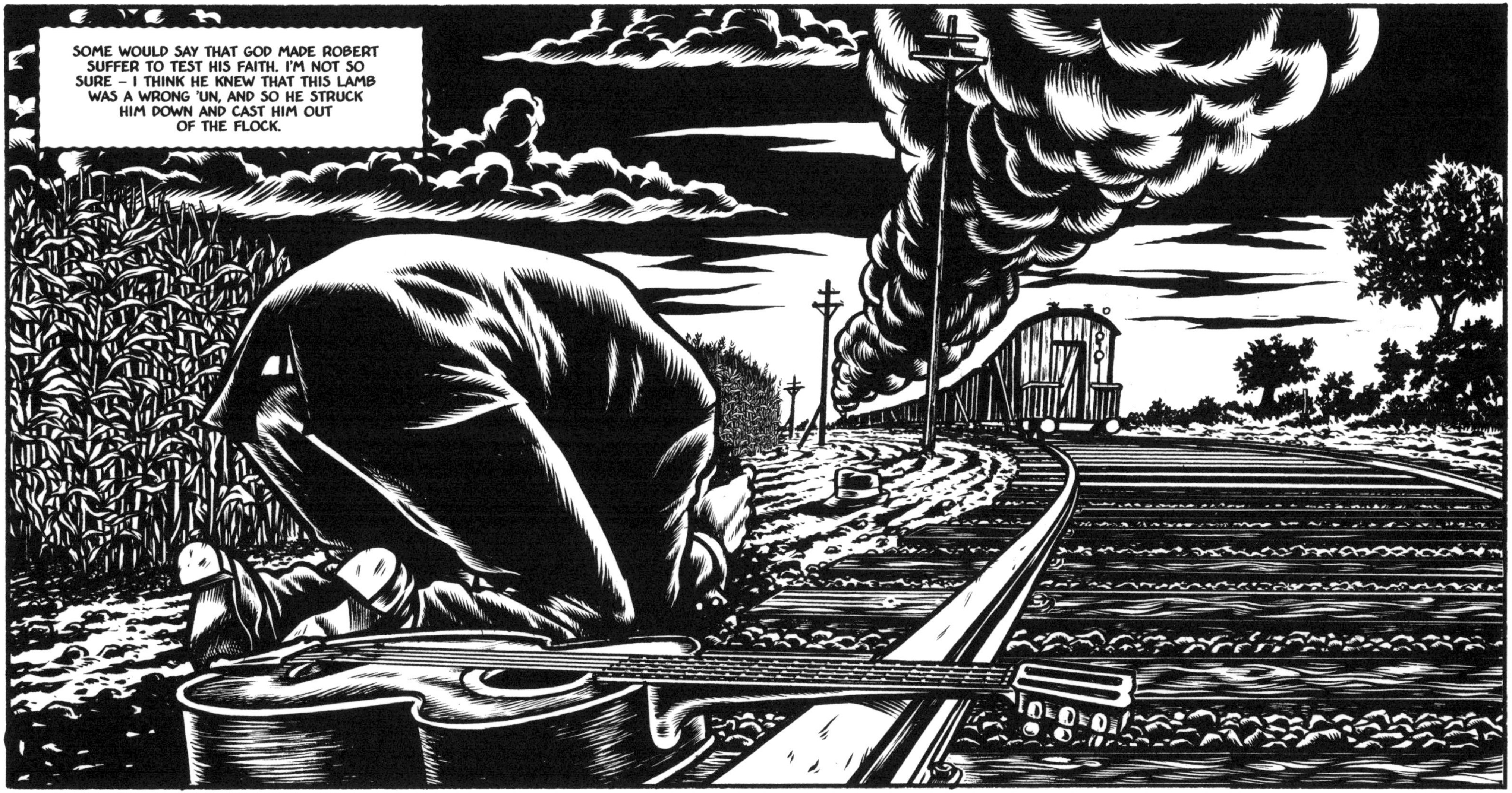
SOME WOULD SAY THAT GOD MADE ROBERT SUFFER TO TEST HIS FAITH. I'M NOT SO SURE – I THINK HE KNEW THAT THIS LAMB WAS A WRONG 'UN, AND SO HE STRUCK HIM DOWN AND CAST HIM OUT OF THE FLOCK.

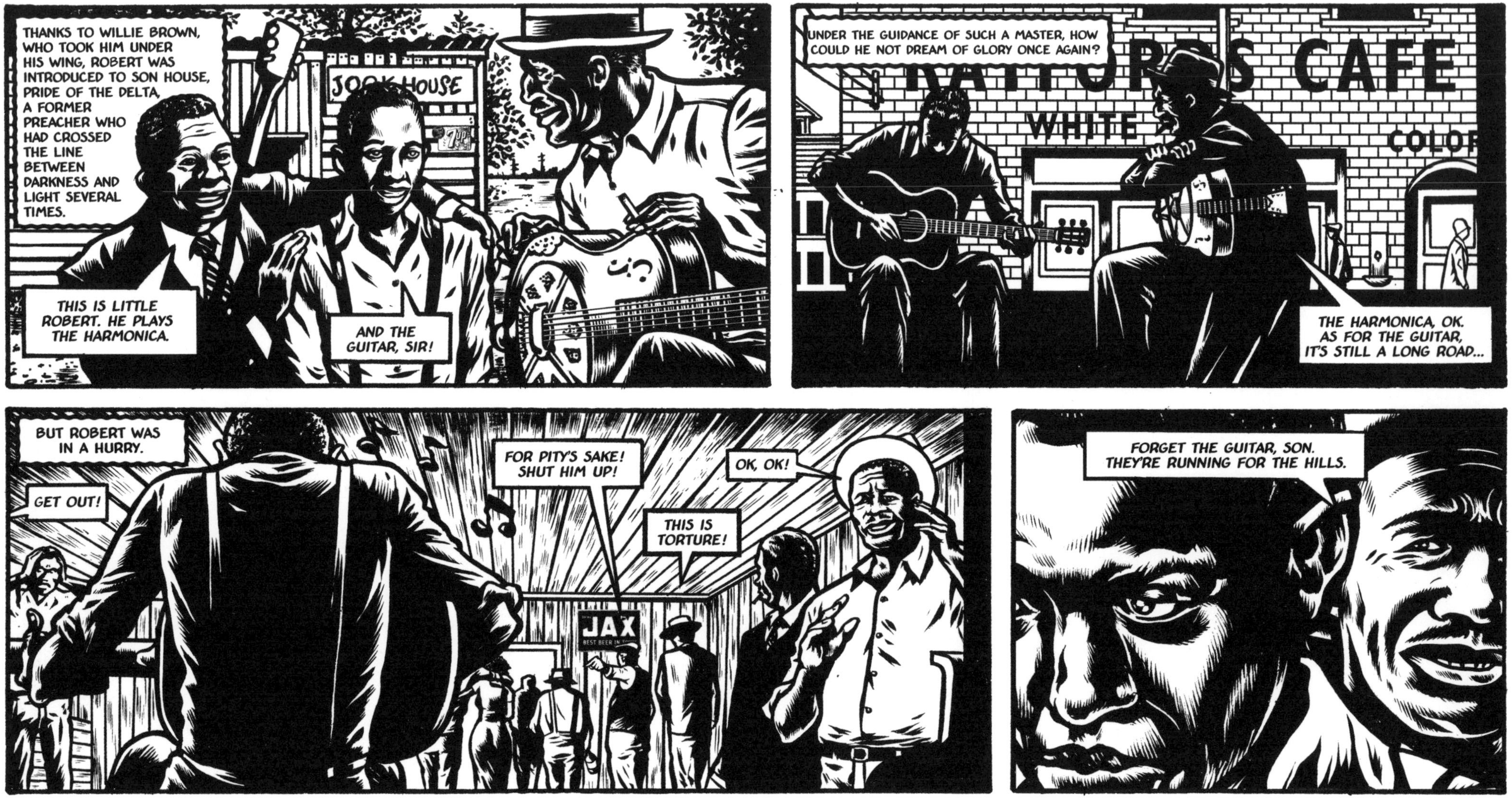
THANKS TO WILLIE BROWN, WHO TOOK HIM UNDER HIS WING, ROBERT WAS INTRODUCED TO SON HOUSE, PRIDE OF THE DELTA, A FORMER PREACHER WHO HAD CROSSED THE LINE BETWEEN DARKNESS AND LIGHT SEVERAL TIMES.
THIS IS LITTLE ROBERT. HE PLAYS THE HARMONICA.
AND THE GUITAR, SIR!
UNDER THE GUIDANCE OF SUCH A MASTER, HOW COULD HE NOT DREAM OF GLORY ONCE AGAIN?
WHITE
THE HARMONICA, OK. AS FOR THE GUITAR, IT'S STILL A LONG ROAD...
BUT ROBERT WAS IN A HURRY.
GET OUT!
FOR PITY'S SAKE! SHUT HIM UP!
THIS IS TORTURE!
OK, OK!
JAX
FORGET THE GUITAR, SON. THEY'RE RUNNING FOR THE HILLS.

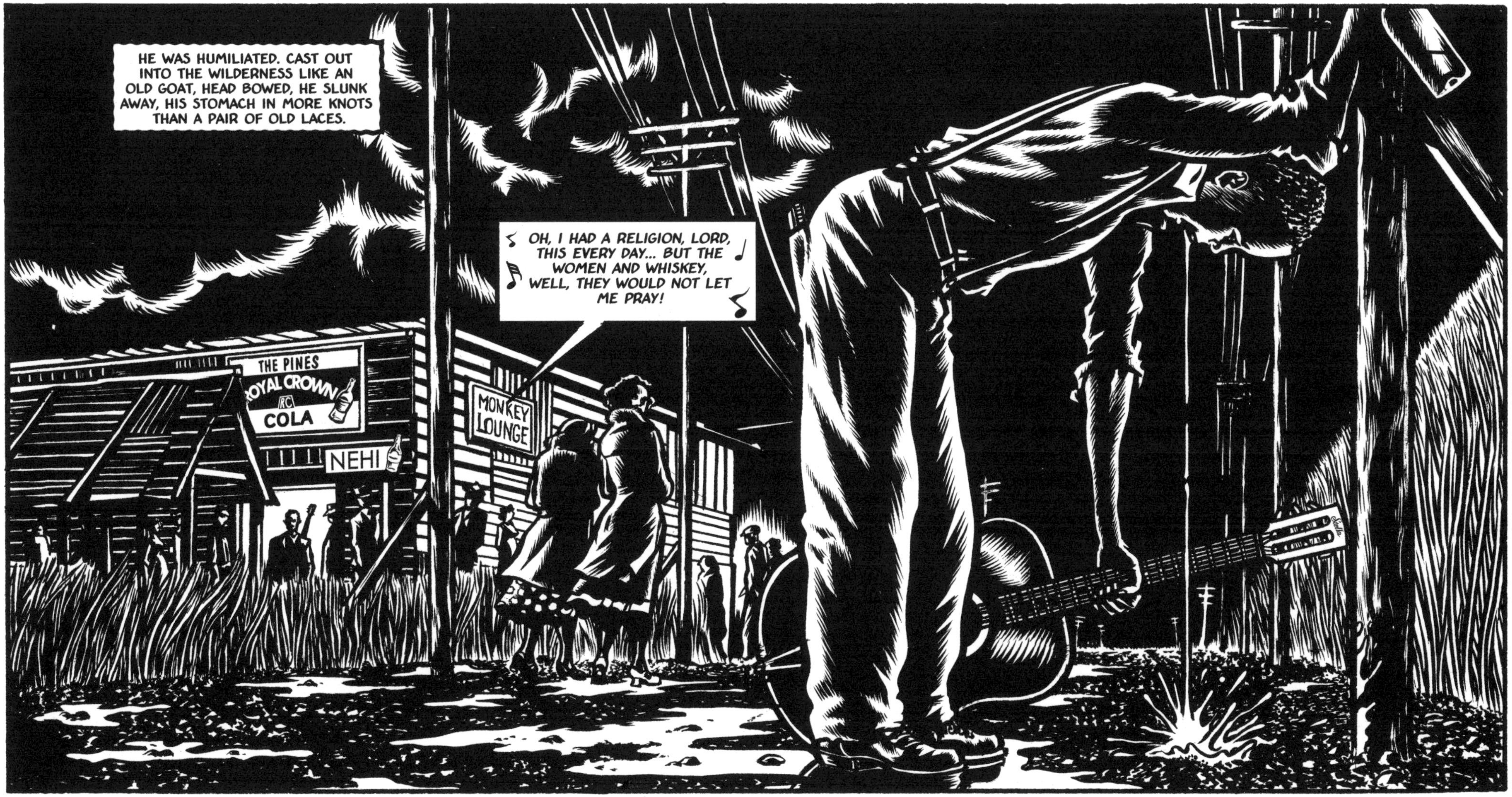
HE WAS HUMILIATED. CAST OUT INTO THE WILDERNESS LIKE AN OLD GOAT, HEAD BOWED, HE SLUNK AWAY, HIS STOMACH IN MORE KNOTS THAN A PAIR OF OLD LACES.
OH, I HAD A RELIGION, LORD, THIS EVERY DAY... BUT THE WOMEN AND WHISKEY, WELL, THEY WOULD NOT LET ME PRAY!
THE PINES
ROYAL CROWN
RC
COLA
NEHI
MONKEY LOUNGE

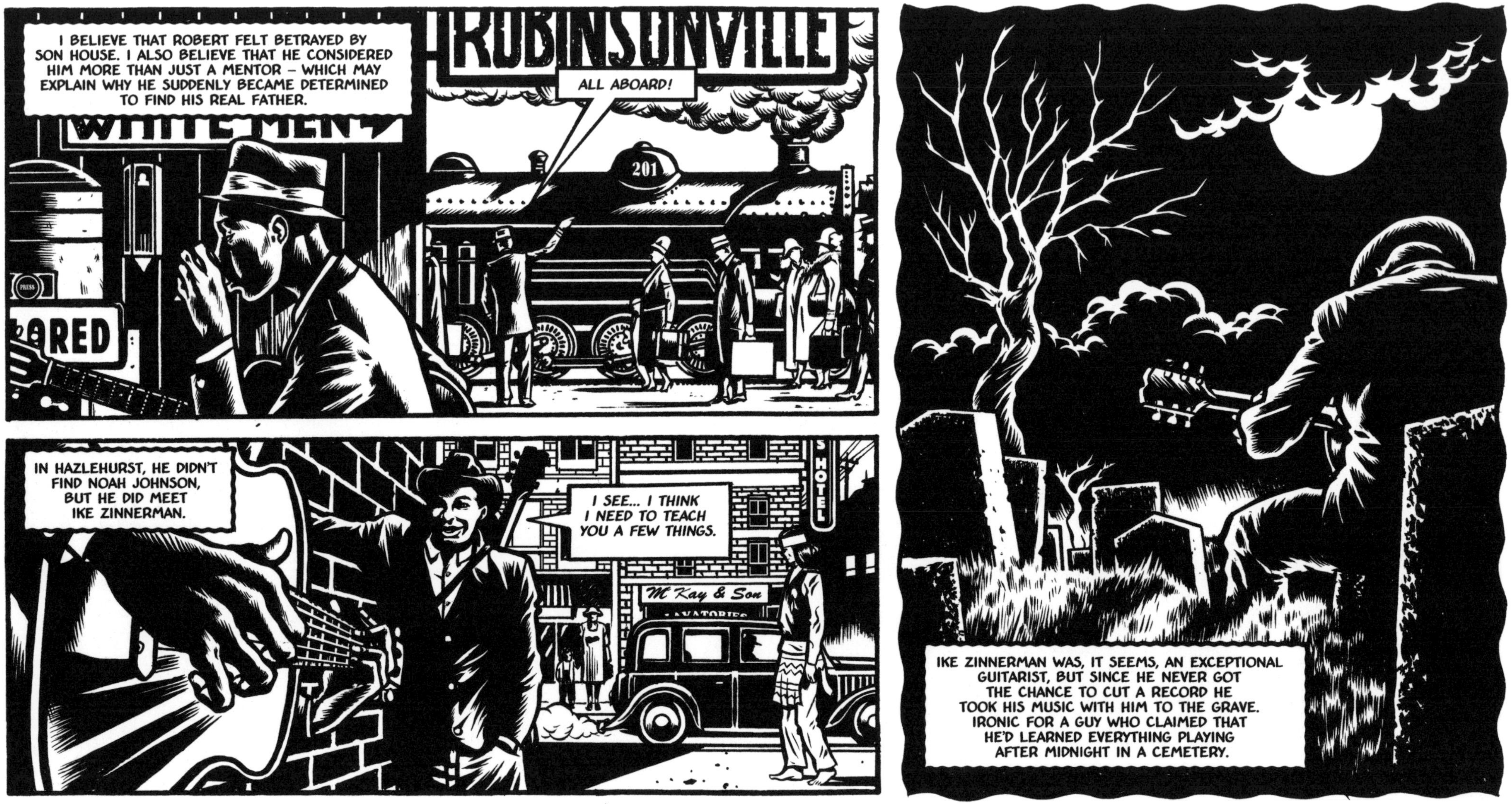
I BELIEVE THAT ROBERT FELT BETRAYED BY SON HOUSE. I ALSO BELIEVE THAT HE CONSIDERED HIM MORE THAN JUST A MENTOR – WHICH MAY EXPLAIN WHY HE SUDDENLY BECAME DETERMINED TO FIND HIS REAL FATHER.
ROBINSONVILLE
ALL ABOARD!
201
IN HAZLEHURST, HE DIDN'T FIND NOAH JOHNSON, BUT HE DID MEET IKE ZINNERMAN.
I SEE... I THINK I NEED TO TEACH YOU A FEW THINGS.
HOTEL
M'Kay & Son
IKE ZINNERMAN WAS, IT SEEMS, AN EXCEPTIONAL GUITARIST, BUT SINCE HE NEVER GOT THE CHANCE TO CUT A RECORD HE TOOK HIS MUSIC WITH HIM TO THE GRAVE. IRONIC FOR A GUY WHO CLAIMED THAT HE'D LEARNED EVERYTHING PLAYING AFTER MIDNIGHT IN A CEMETERY.

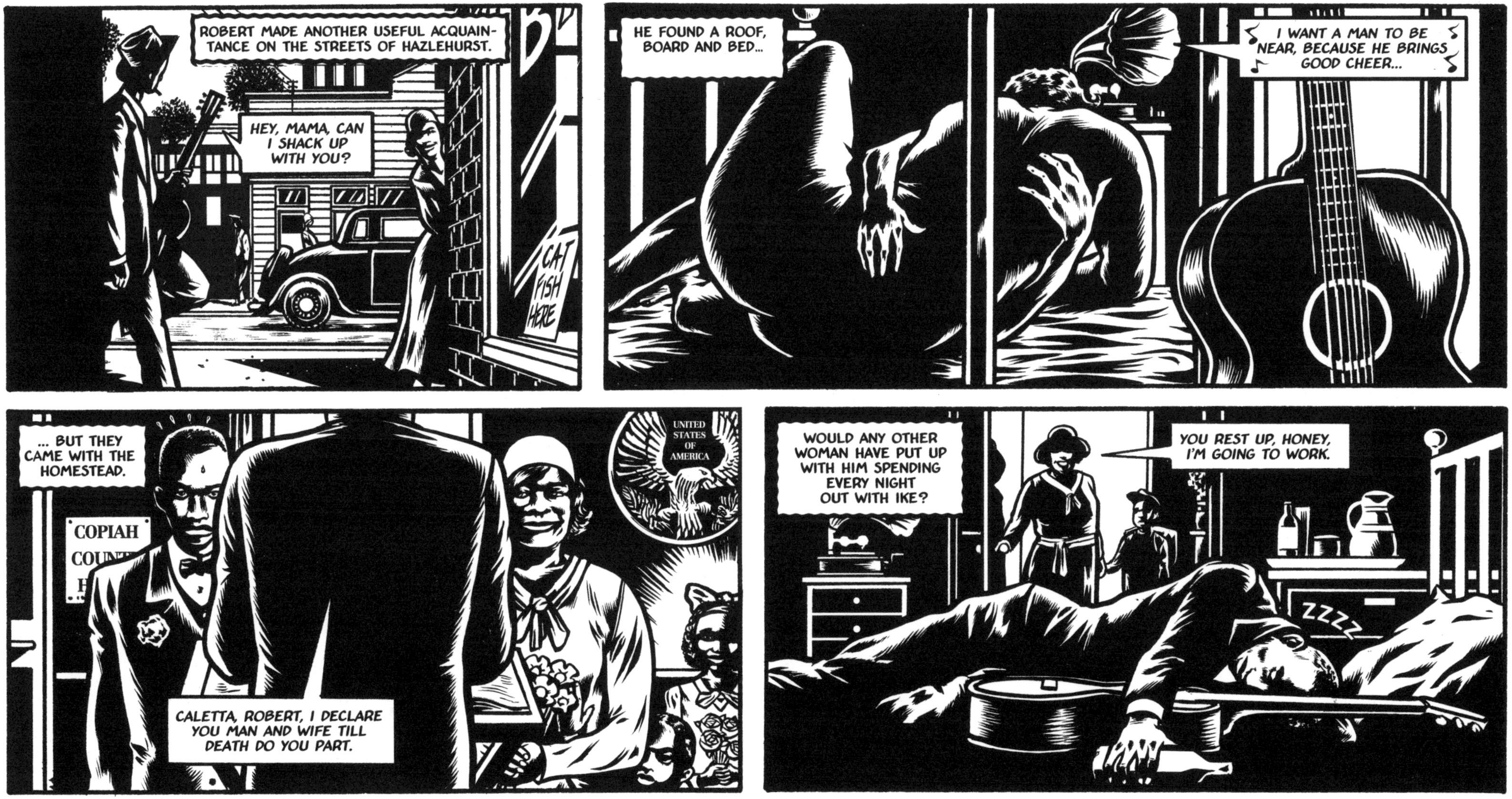
ROBERT MADE ANOTHER USEFUL ACQUAINTANCE ON THE STREETS OF HAZLEHURST.
HEY, MAMA, CAN I SHACK UP WITH YOU?
CAT FISH HERE
HE FOUND A ROOF, BOARD AND BED...
I WANT A MAN TO BE NEAR, BECAUSE HE BRINGS GOOD CHEER...
... BUT THEY CAME WITH THE HOMESTEAD.
COPIAH
UNITED STATES OF AMERICA
CALETTA, ROBERT, I DECLARE YOU MAN AND WIFE TILL DEATH DO YOU PART.
WOULD ANY OTHER WOMAN HAVE PUT UP WITH HIM SPENDING EVERY NIGHT OUT WITH IKE?
YOU REST UP, HONEY, I'M GOING TO WORK.
ZZZZ

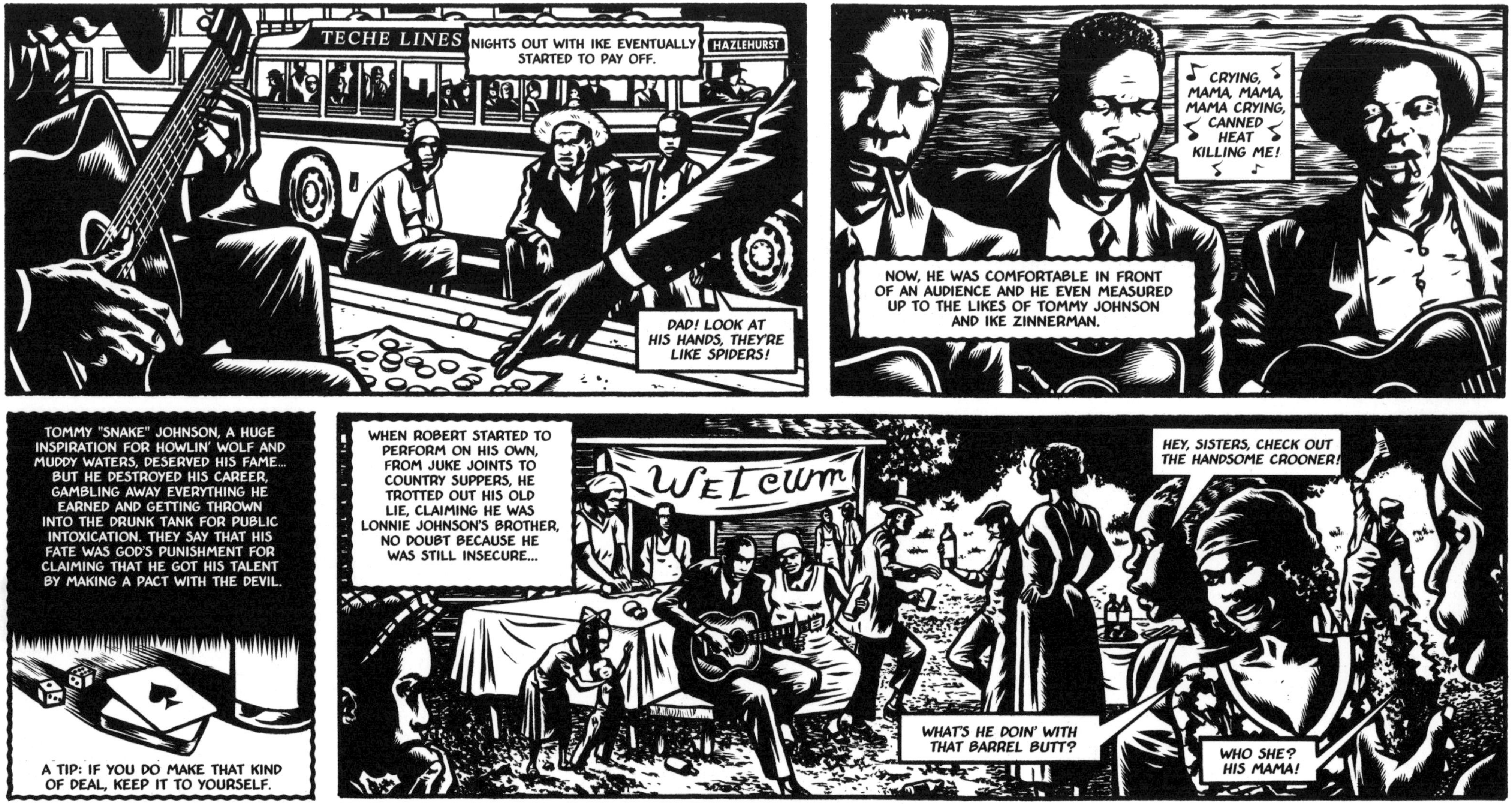
TECHE LINES
NIGHTS OUT WITH IKE EVENTUALLY STARTED TO PAY OFF.
HAZLEHURST
DAD! LOOK AT HIS HANDS, THEY'RE LIKE SPIDERS!
CRYING, MAMA, MAMA, MAMA CRYING, CANNED HEAT KILLING ME!
NOW, HE WAS COMFORTABLE IN FRONT OF AN AUDIENCE AND HE EVEN MEASURED UP TO THE LIKES OF TOMMY JOHNSON AND IKE ZINNERMAN.
TOMMY "SNAKE" JOHNSON, A HUGE INSPIRATION FOR HOWLIN' WOLF AND MUDDY WATERS, DESERVED HIS FAME... BUT HE DESTROYED HIS CAREER, GAMBLING AWAY EVERYTHING HE EARNED AND GETTING THROWN INTO THE DRUNK TANK FOR PUBLIC INTOXICATION. THEY SAY THAT HIS FATE WAS GOD'S PUNISHMENT FOR CLAIMING THAT HE GOT HIS TALENT BY MAKING A PACT WITH THE DEVIL.
A TIP: IF YOU DO MAKE THAT KIND OF DEAL, KEEP IT TO YOURSELF.
WHEN ROBERT STARTED TO PERFORM ON HIS OWN, FROM JUKE JOINTS TO COUNTRY SUPPERS, HE TROTTED OUT HIS OLD LIE, CLAIMING HE WAS LONNIE JOHNSON'S BROTHER, NO DOUBT BECAUSE HE WAS STILL INSECURE...
WELCUM
HEY, SISTERS, CHECK OUT THE HANDSOME CROONER!
WHAT'S HE DOIN' WITH THAT BARREL BUTT?
WHO SHE? HIS MAMA!

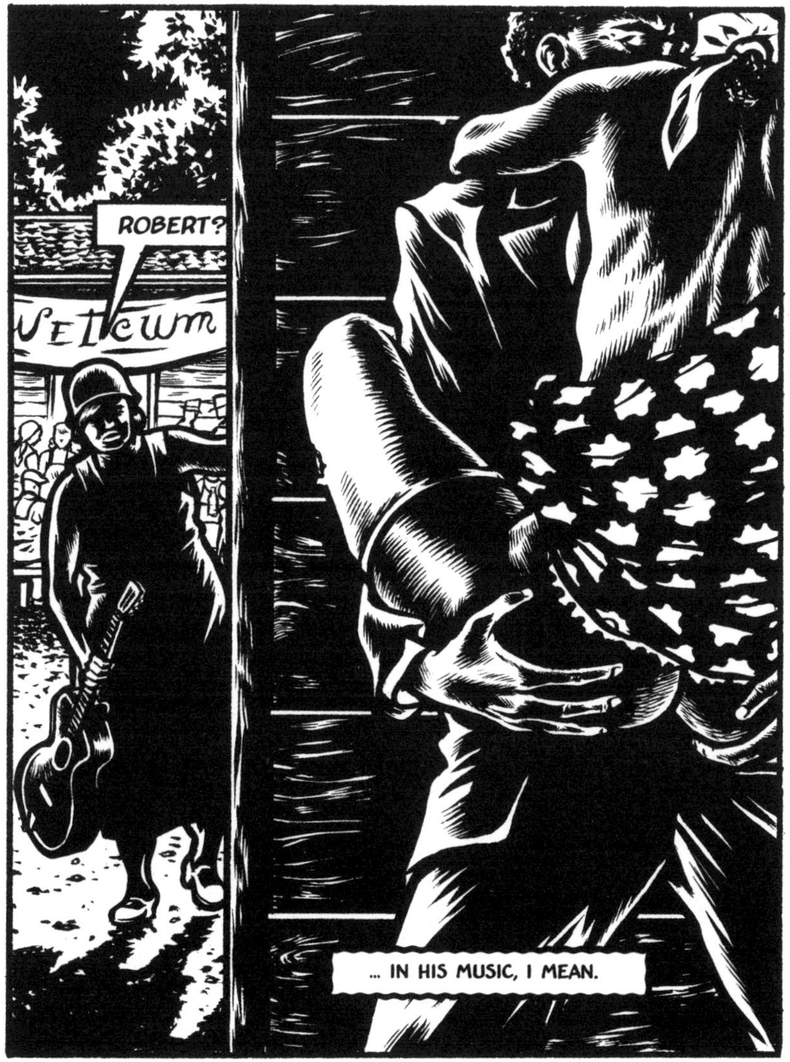
ROBERT?
... IN HIS MUSIC, I MEAN.

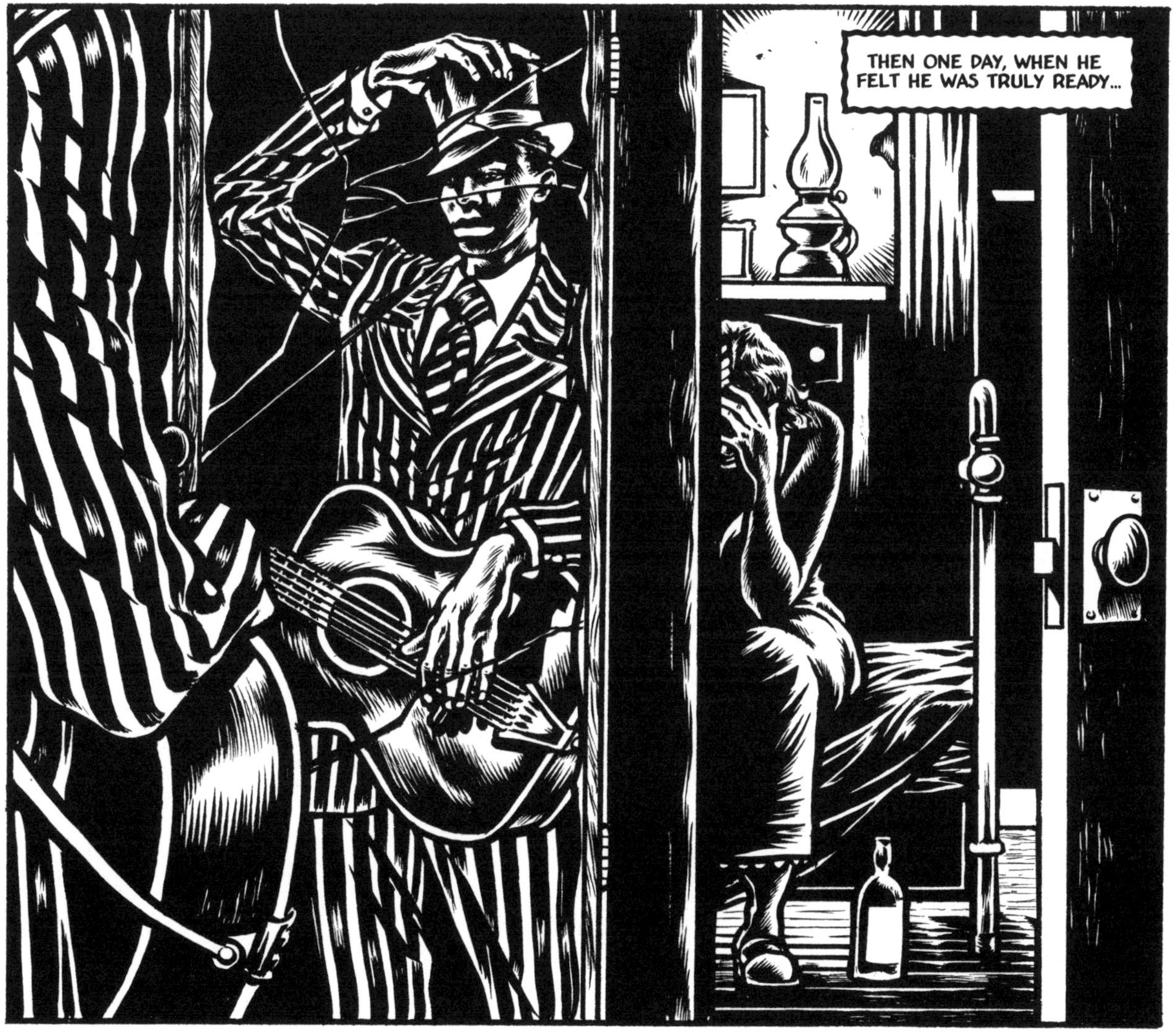
THEN ONE DAY, WHEN HE FELT HE WAS TRULY READY...

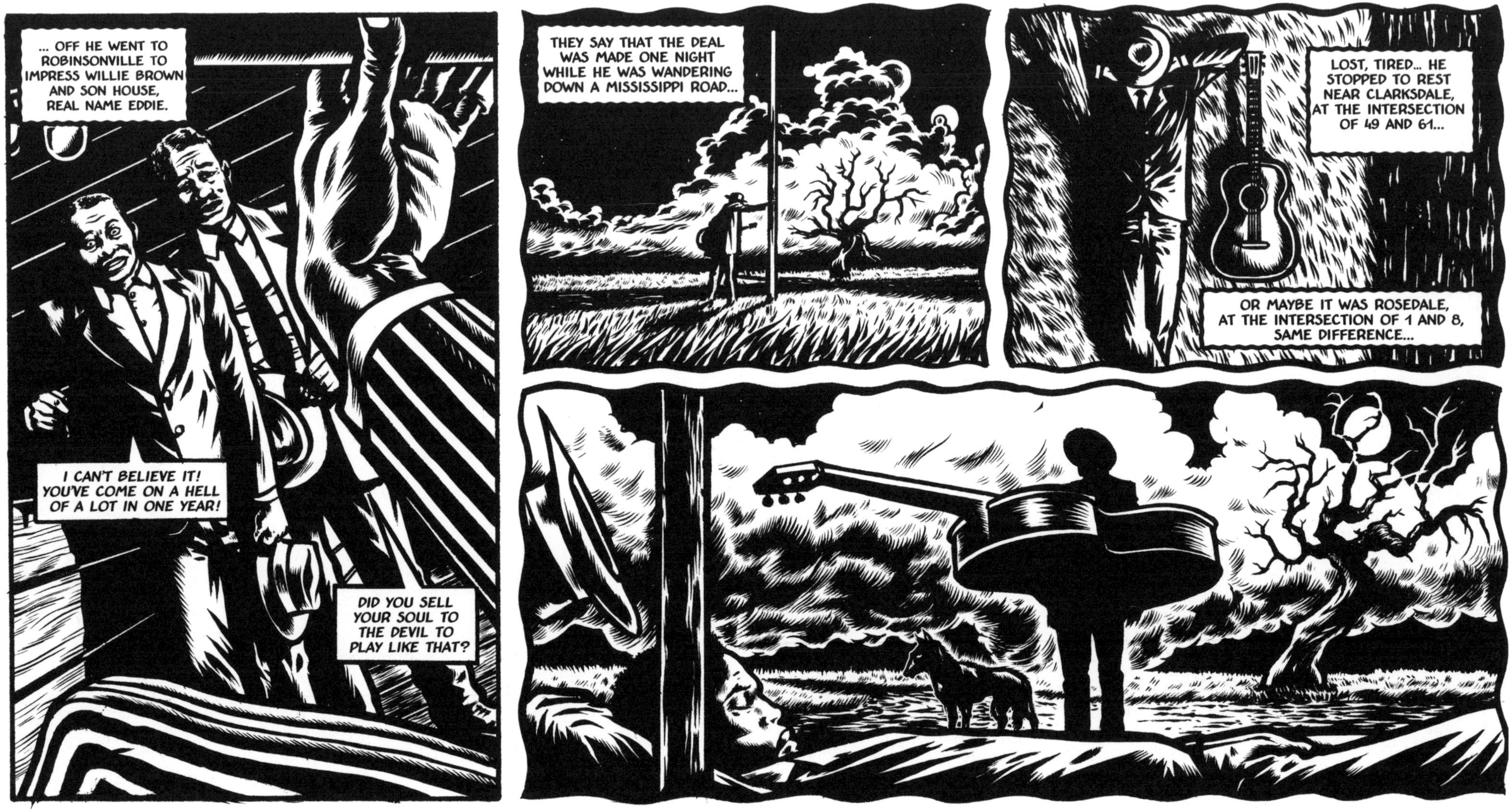
... OFF HE WENT TO ROBINSONVILLE TO IMPRESS WILLIE BROWN AND SON HOUSE, REAL NAME EDDIE.
I CAN'T BELIEVE IT! YOU'VE COME ON A HELL OF A LOT IN ONE YEAR!
DID YOU SELL YOUR SOUL TO THE DEVIL TO PLAY LIKE THAT?
THEY SAY THAT THE DEAL WAS MADE ONE NIGHT WHILE HE WAS WANDERING DOWN A MISSISSIPPI ROAD...
LOST, TIRED... HE STOPPED TO REST NEAR CLARKSDALE, AT THE INTERSECTION OF 49 AND 61...
OR MAYBE IT WAS ROSEDALE, AT THE INTERSECTION OF 1 AND 8, SAME DIFFERENCE...

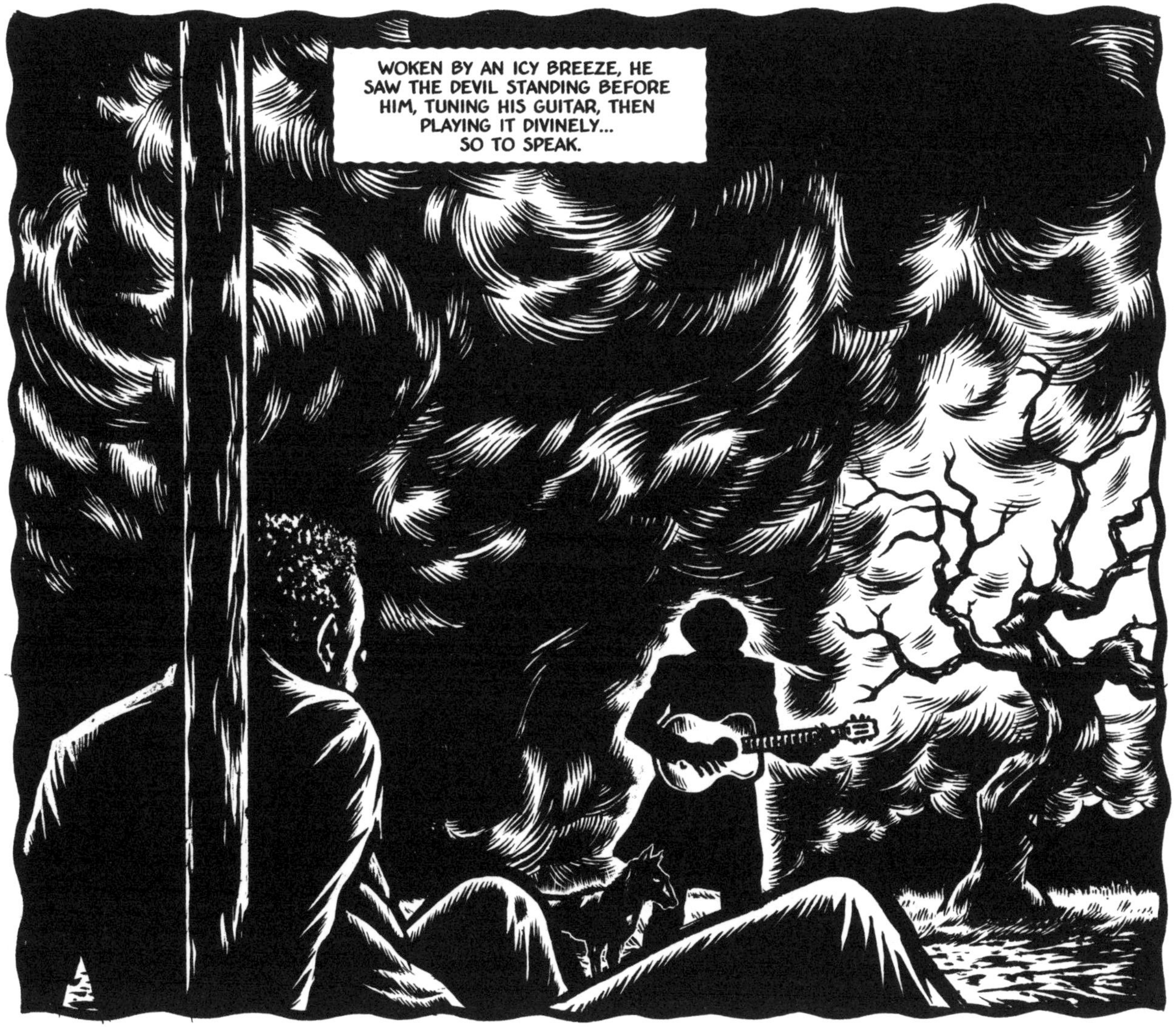
WOKEN BY AN ICY BREEZE, HE SAW THE DEVIL STANDING BEFORE HIM, TUNING HIS GUITAR, THEN PLAYING IT DIVINELY... SO TO SPEAK.

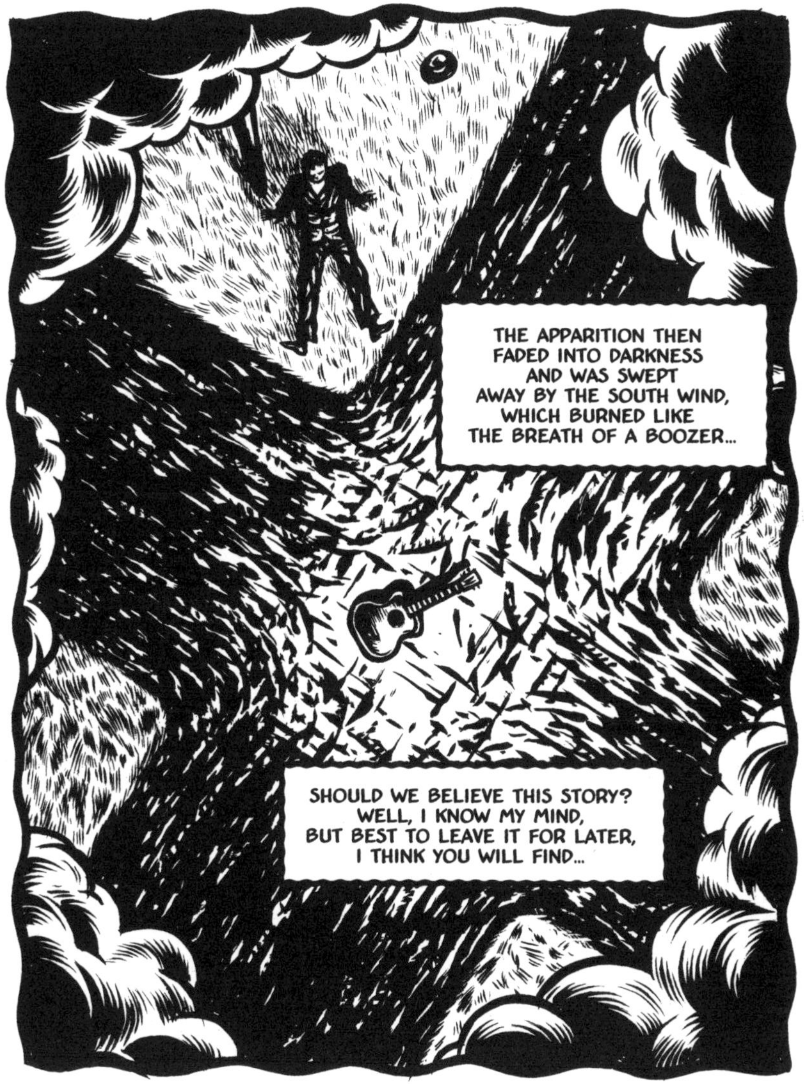
THE APPARITION THEN FADED INTO DARKNESS AND WAS SWEPT AWAY BY THE SOUTH WIND, WHICH BURNED LIKE THE BREATH OF A BOOZER...
SHOULD WE BELIEVE THIS STORY? WELL, I KNOW MY MIND, BUT BEST TO LEAVE IT FOR LATER, I THINK YOU WILL FIND...

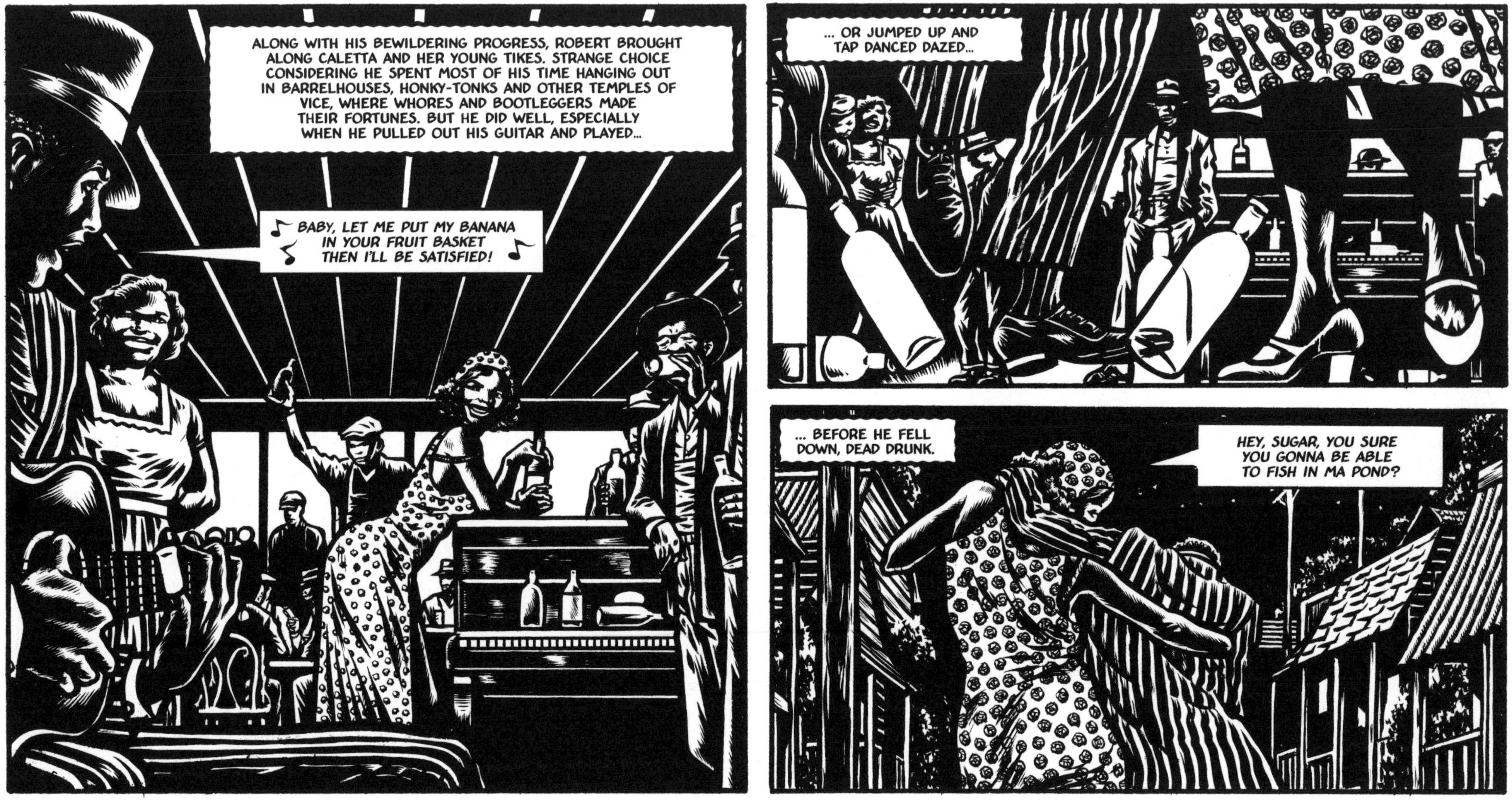
ALONG WITH HIS BEWILDERING PROGRESS, ROBERT BROUGHT ALONG CALETTA AND HER YOUNG TIKES. STRANGE CHOICE CONSIDERING HE SPENT MOST OF HIS TIME HANGING OUT IN BARRELHOUSES, HONKY-TONKS AND OTHER TEMPLES OF VICE, WHERE WHORES AND BOOTLEGGERS MADE THEIR FORTUNES. BUT HE DID WELL, ESPECIALLY WHEN HE PULLED OUT HIS GUITAR AND PLAYED...
BABY, LET ME PUT MY BANANA IN YOUR FRUIT BASKET THEN I'LL BE SATISFIED!
... OR JUMPED UP AND TAP DANCED DAZED...
... BEFORE HE FELL DOWN, DEAD DRUNK.
HEY, SUGAR, YOU SURE YOU GONNA BE ABLE TO FISH IN MA POND?

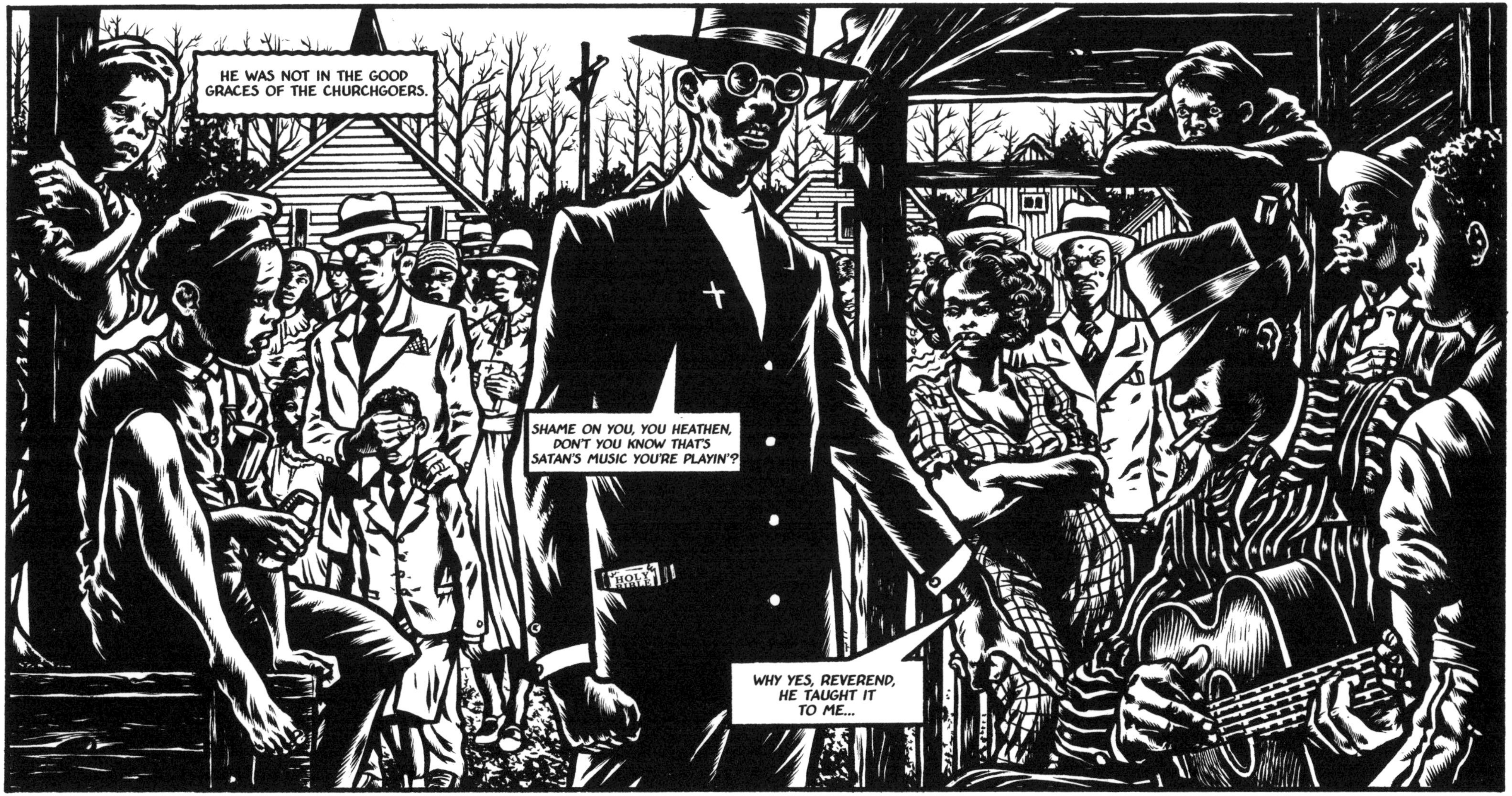
HE WAS NOT IN THE GOOD GRACES OF THE CHURCHGOERS.
SHAME ON YOU, YOU HEATHEN, DON'T YOU KNOW THAT'S SATAN'S MUSIC YOU'RE PLAYIN'?
WHY YES, REVEREND, HE TAUGHT IT TO ME...
HOLY BIBLE

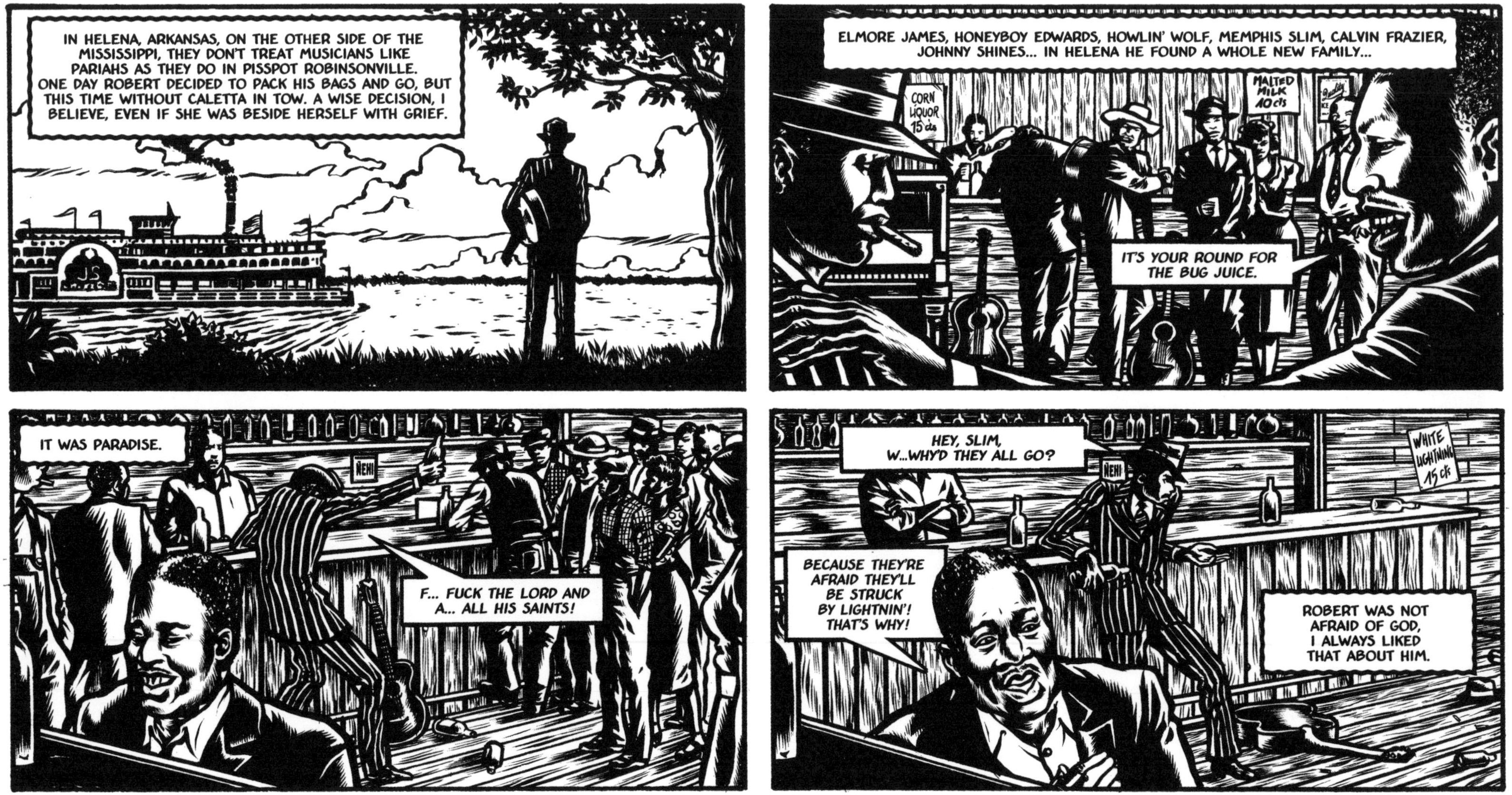
IN HELENA, ARKANSAS, ON THE OTHER SIDE OF THE MISSISSIPPI, THEY DON'T TREAT MUSICIANS LIKE PARIAHS AS THEY DO IN PISSPOT ROBINSONVILLE. ONE DAY ROBERT DECIDED TO PACK HIS BAGS AND GO, BUT THIS TIME WITHOUT CALETTA IN TOW. A WISE DECISION, I BELIEVE, EVEN IF SHE WAS BESIDE HERSELF WITH GRIEF.
JS
ELMORE JAMES, HONEYBOY EDWARDS, HOWLIN' WOLF, MEMPHIS SLIM, CALVIN FRAZIER, JOHNNY SHINES... IN HELENA HE FOUND A WHOLE NEW FAMILY...
CORN LIQUOR 15 cts
MALTED MILK 10 cts
IT'S YOUR ROUND FOR THE BUG JUICE.
IT WAS PARADISE.
NEHI
F... FUCK THE LORD AND A... ALL HIS SAINTS!
HEY, SLIM, W...WHY'D THEY ALL GO?
NEHI
WHITE LIGHTNING 15 cts
BECAUSE THEY'RE AFRAID THEY'LL BE STRUCK BY LIGHTNIN'! THAT'S WHY!
ROBERT WAS NOT AFRAID OF GOD, I ALWAYS LIKED THAT ABOUT HIM.

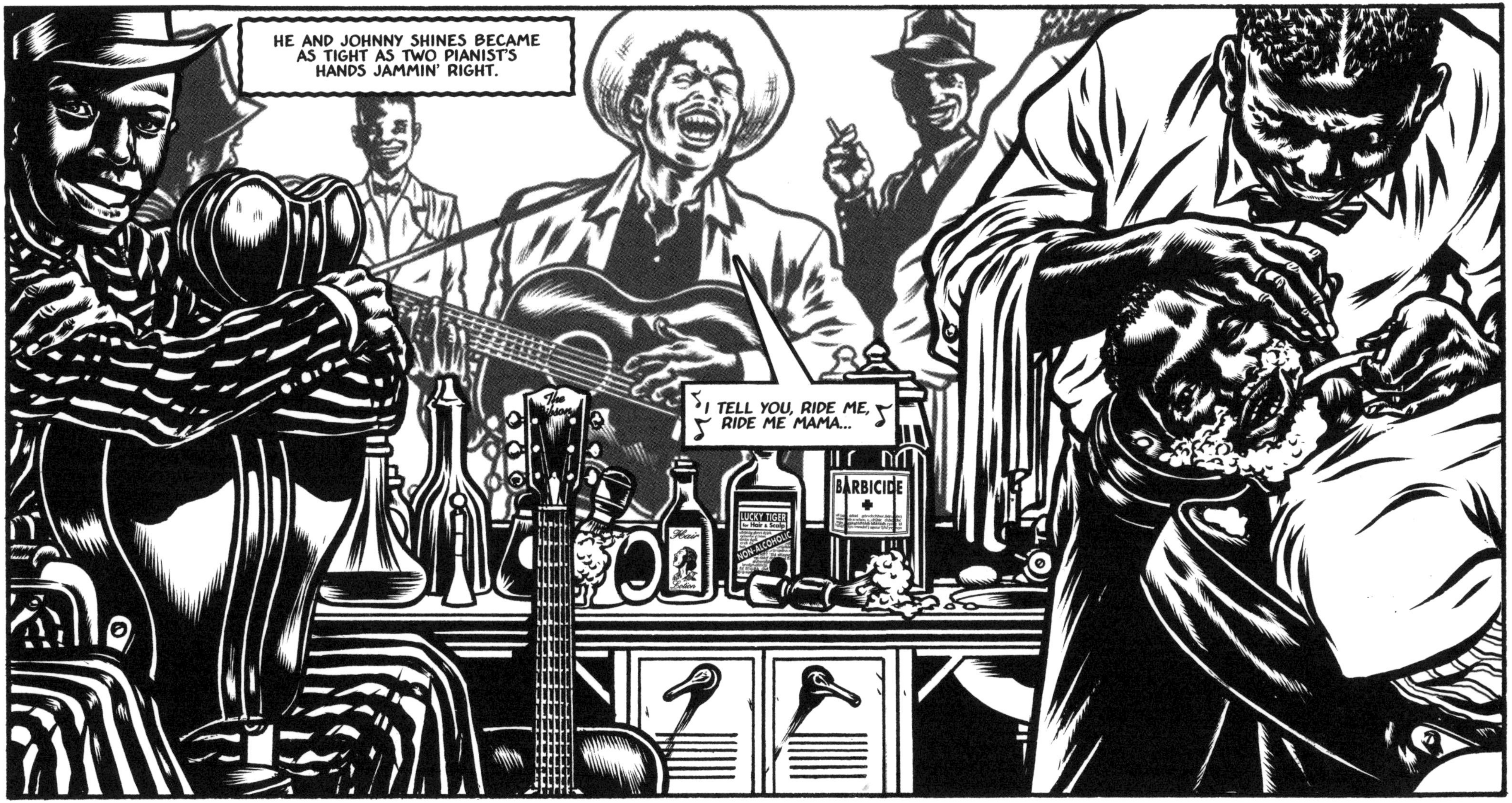
HE AND JOHNNY SHINES BECAME AS TIGHT AS TWO PIANIST'S HANDS JAMMIN' RIGHT.
I TELL YOU, RIDE ME, RIDE ME MAMA...
LUCKY TIGER for Hair & Scalp
NON-ALCOHOLIC
BARBICIDE
Hair Lotion

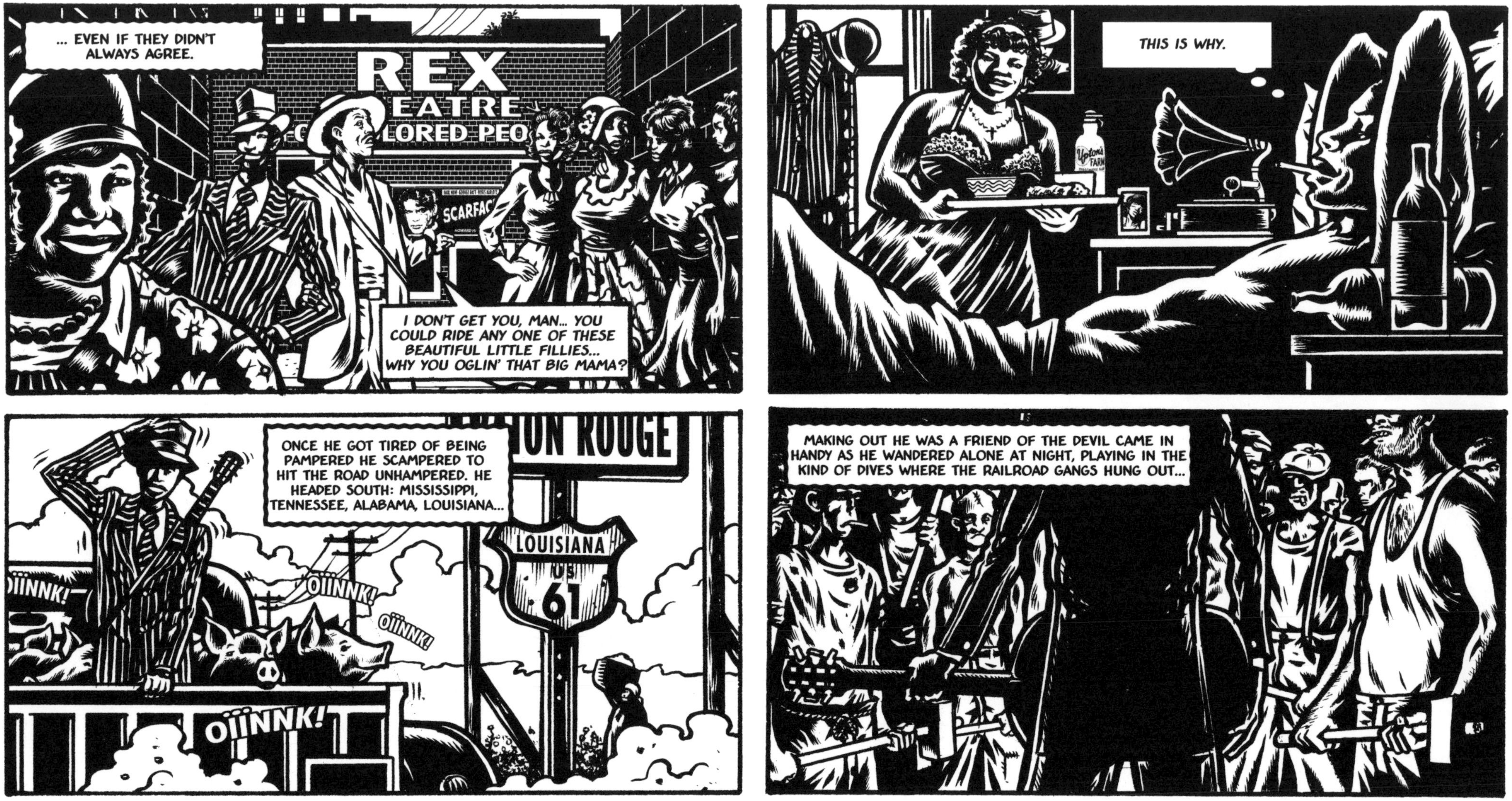
... EVEN IF THEY DIDN'T ALWAYS AGREE.
REX
EATRE
LORED PEO
SCARFAC
I DON'T GET YOU, MAN... YOU COULD RIDE ANY ONE OF THESE BEAUTIFUL LITTLE FILLIES... WHY YOU OGLIN' THAT BIG MAMA?
THIS IS WHY.
Upton's FARM
ONCE HE GOT TIRED OF BEING PAMPERED HE SCAMPERED TO HIT THE ROAD UNHAMPERED. HE HEADED SOUTH: MISSISSIPPI, TENNESSEE, ALABAMA, LOUISIANA...
ON ROUGE
LOUISIANA
US
61
OÏINNK!
OÏINNK!
OÏINNK!
OÏINNK!
MAKING OUT HE WAS A FRIEND OF THE DEVIL CAME IN HANDY AS HE WANDERED ALONE AT NIGHT, PLAYING IN THE KIND OF DIVES WHERE THE RAILROAD GANGS HUNG OUT...

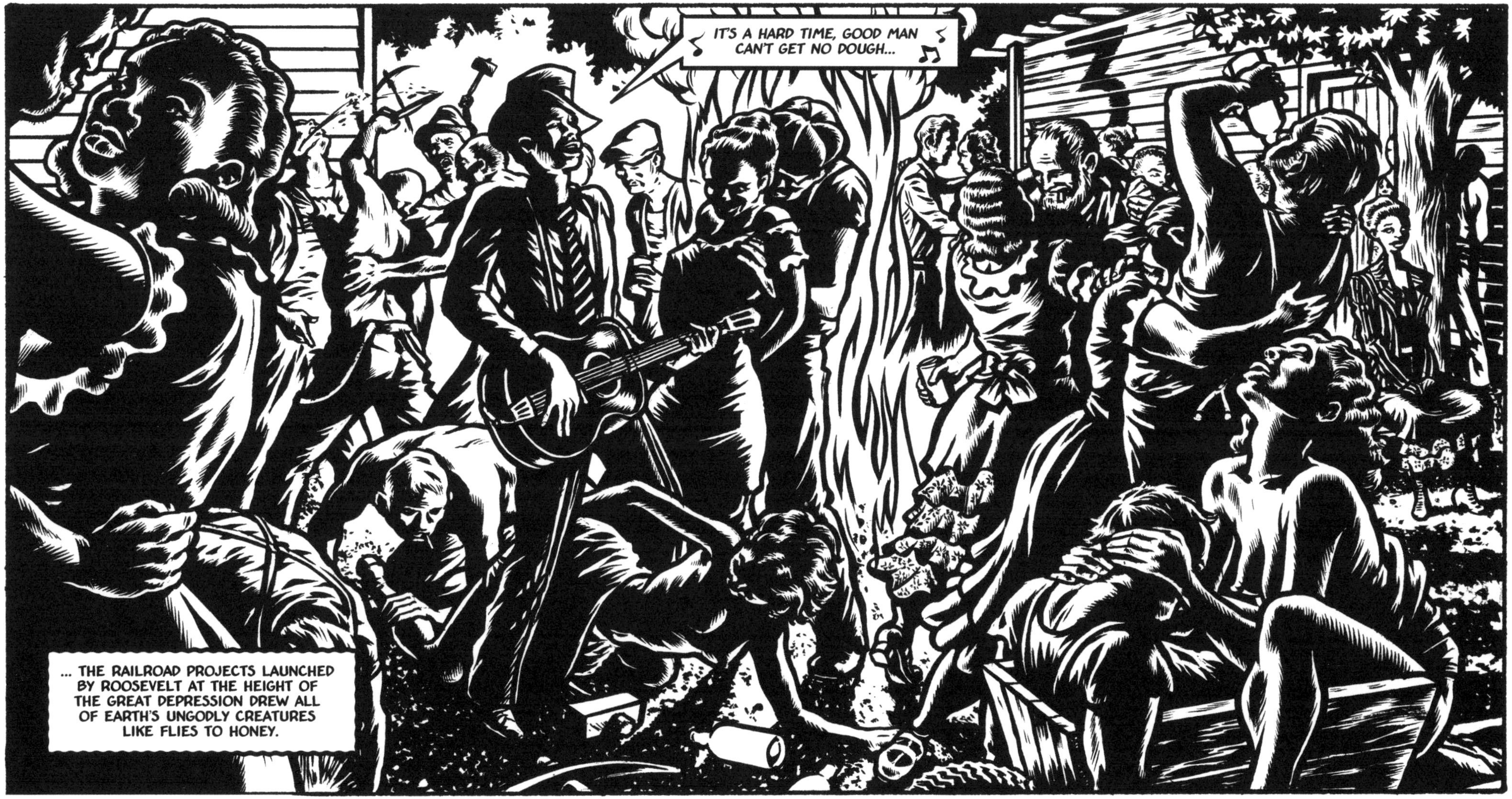
IT'S A HARD TIME, GOOD MAN
CAN'T GET NO DOUGH...
... THE RAILROAD PROJECTS LAUNCHED
BY ROOSEVELT AT THE HEIGHT OF
THE GREAT DEPRESSION DREW ALL
OF EARTH'S UNGODLY CREATURES
LIKE FLIES TO HONEY.

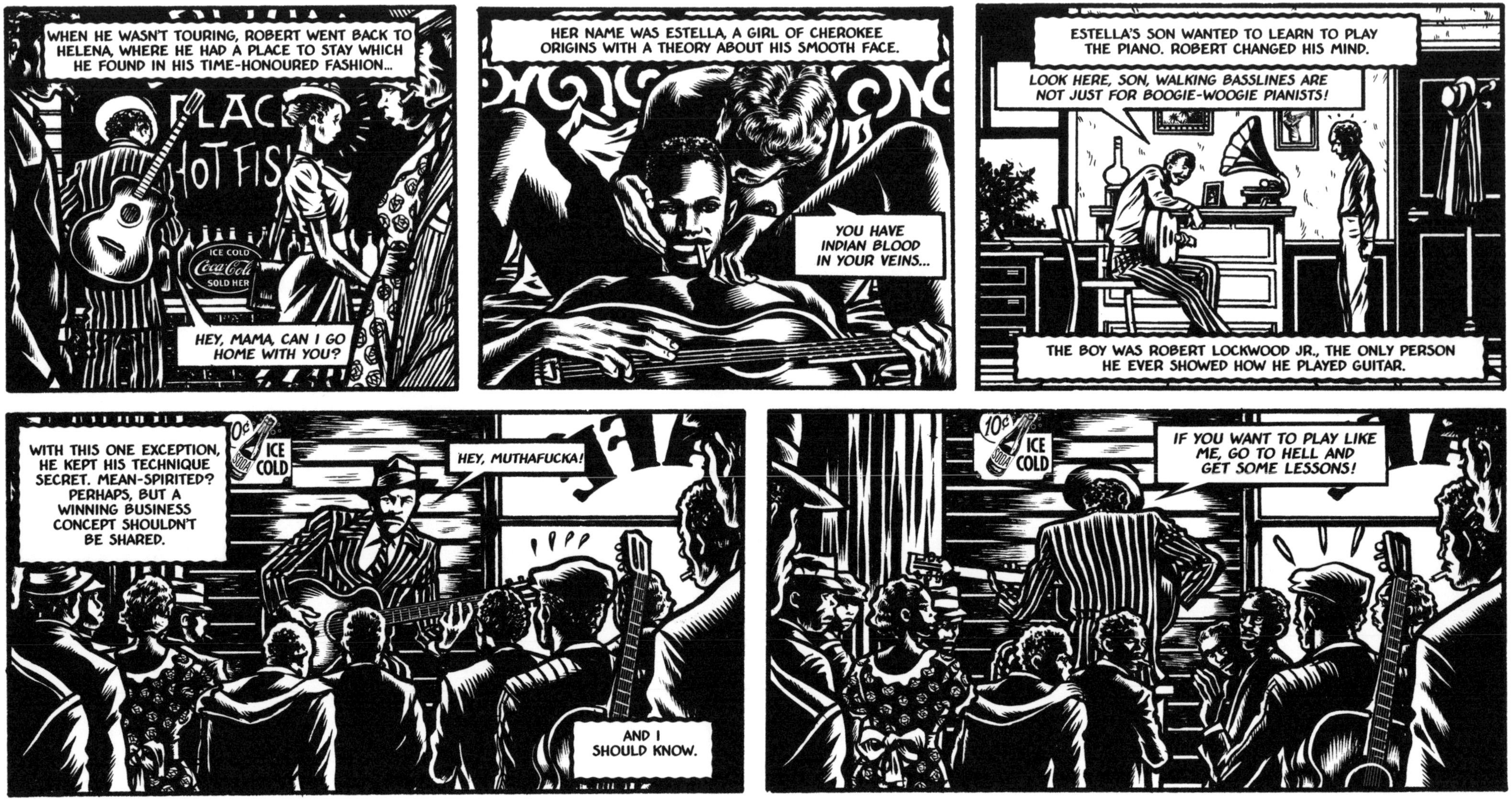

WHEN HE WASN'T TOURING, ROBERT WENT BACK TO HELENA, WHERE HE HAD A PLACE TO STAY WHICH HE FOUND IN HIS TIME-HONOURED FASHION...
ICE COLD
SOLD HER
HEY, MAMA, CAN I GO HOME WITH YOU?
HER NAME WAS ESTELLA, A GIRL OF CHEROKEE ORIGINS WITH A THEORY ABOUT HIS SMOOTH FACE.
YOU HAVE INDIAN BLOOD IN YOUR VEINS...
ESTELLA'S SON WANTED TO LEARN TO PLAY THE PIANO. ROBERT CHANGED HIS MIND.
LOOK HERE, SON, WALKING BASSLINES ARE NOT JUST FOR BOOGIE-WOOGIE PIANISTS!
THE BOY WAS ROBERT LOCKWOOD JR., THE ONLY PERSON HE EVER SHOWED HOW HE PLAYED GUITAR.
WITH THIS ONE EXCEPTION, HE KEPT HIS TECHNIQUE SECRET. MEAN-SPIRITED? PERHAPS, BUT A WINNING BUSINESS CONCEPT SHOULDN'T BE SHARED.
10¢ SODA
ICE COLD
HEY, MUTHAFUCKA!
AND I SHOULD KNOW.
10¢ SODA
ICE COLD
IF YOU WANT TO PLAY LIKE ME, GO TO HELL AND GET SOME LESSONS!

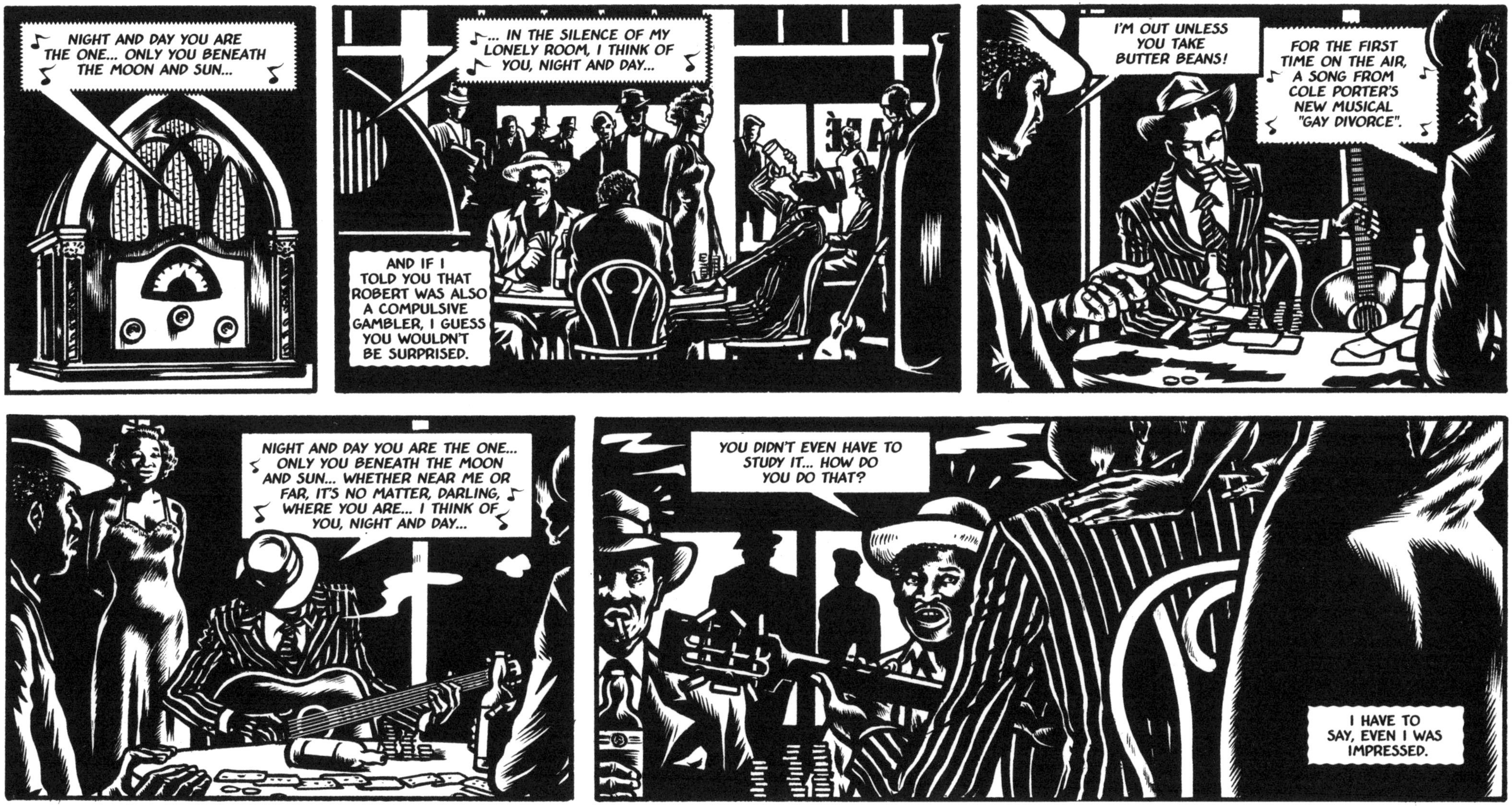
NIGHT AND DAY YOU ARE THE ONE... ONLY YOU BENEATH THE MOON AND SUN...
... IN THE SILENCE OF MY LONELY ROOM, I THINK OF YOU, NIGHT AND DAY...
AND IF I TOLD YOU THAT ROBERT WAS ALSO A COMPULSIVE GAMBLER, I GUESS YOU WOULDN'T BE SURPRISED.
I'M OUT UNLESS YOU TAKE BUTTER BEANS!
FOR THE FIRST TIME ON THE AIR, A SONG FROM COLE PORTER'S NEW MUSICAL "GAY DIVORCE".
NIGHT AND DAY YOU ARE THE ONE... ONLY YOU BENEATH THE MOON AND SUN... WHETHER NEAR ME OR FAR, IT'S NO MATTER, DARLING, WHERE YOU ARE... I THINK OF YOU, NIGHT AND DAY...
YOU DIDN'T EVEN HAVE TO STUDY IT... HOW DO YOU DO THAT?
I HAVE TO SAY, EVEN I WAS IMPRESSED.

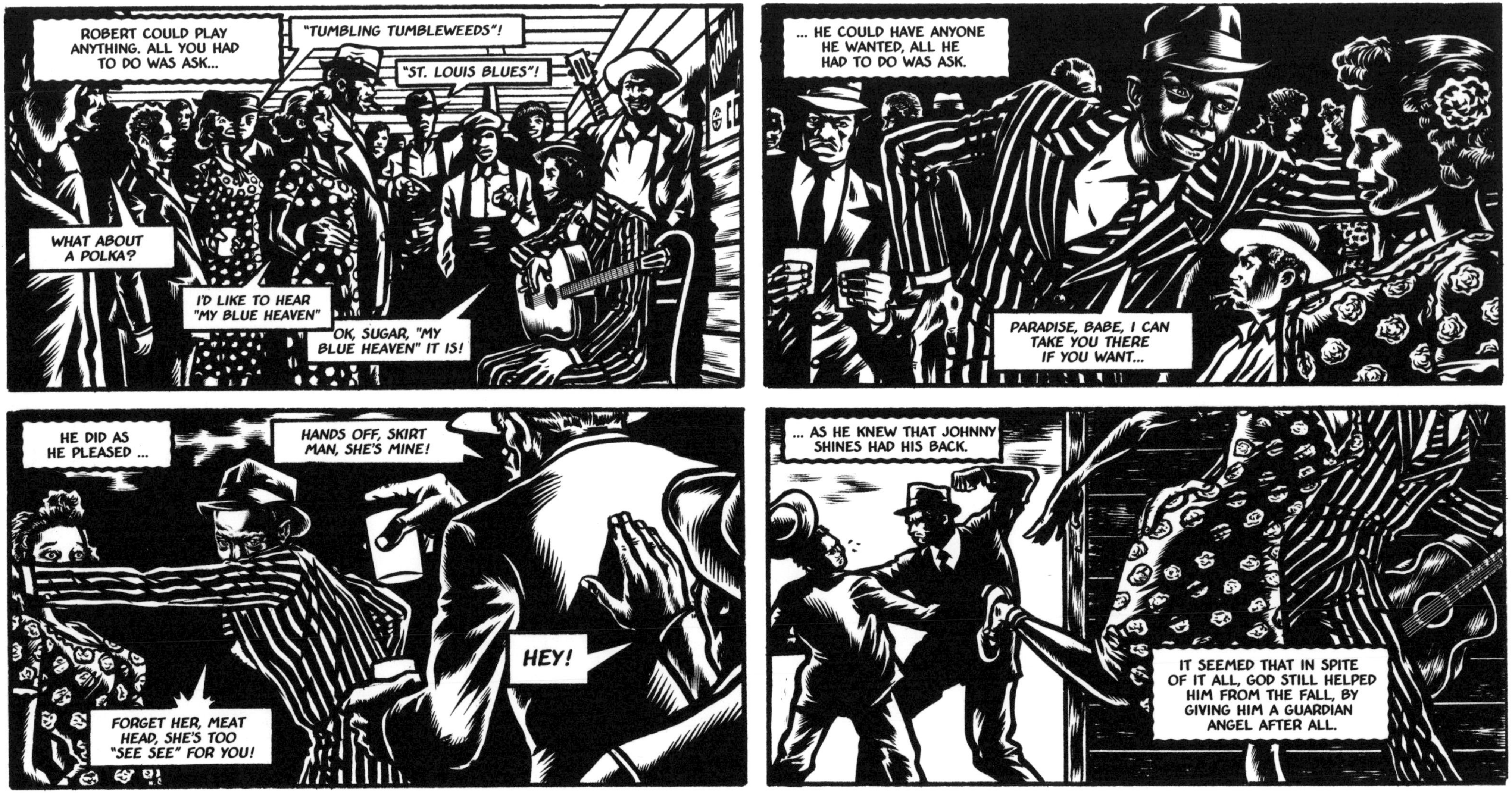
ROBERT COULD PLAY ANYTHING. ALL YOU HAD TO DO WAS ASK...
"TUMBLING TUMBLEWEEDS"!
"ST. LOUIS BLUES"!
WHAT ABOUT A POLKA?
I'D LIKE TO HEAR "MY BLUE HEAVEN"
OK, SUGAR, "MY BLUE HEAVEN" IT IS!
... HE COULD HAVE ANYONE HE WANTED, ALL HE HAD TO DO WAS ASK.
PARADISE, BABE, I CAN TAKE YOU THERE IF YOU WANT...
HE DID AS HE PLEASED ...
HANDS OFF, SKIRT MAN, SHE'S MINE!
HEY!
FORGET HER, MEAT HEAD, SHE'S TOO "SEE SEE" FOR YOU!
... AS HE KNEW THAT JOHNNY SHINES HAD HIS BACK.
IT SEEMED THAT IN SPITE OF IT ALL, GOD STILL HELPED HIM FROM THE FALL, BY GIVING HIM A GUARDIAN ANGEL AFTER ALL.

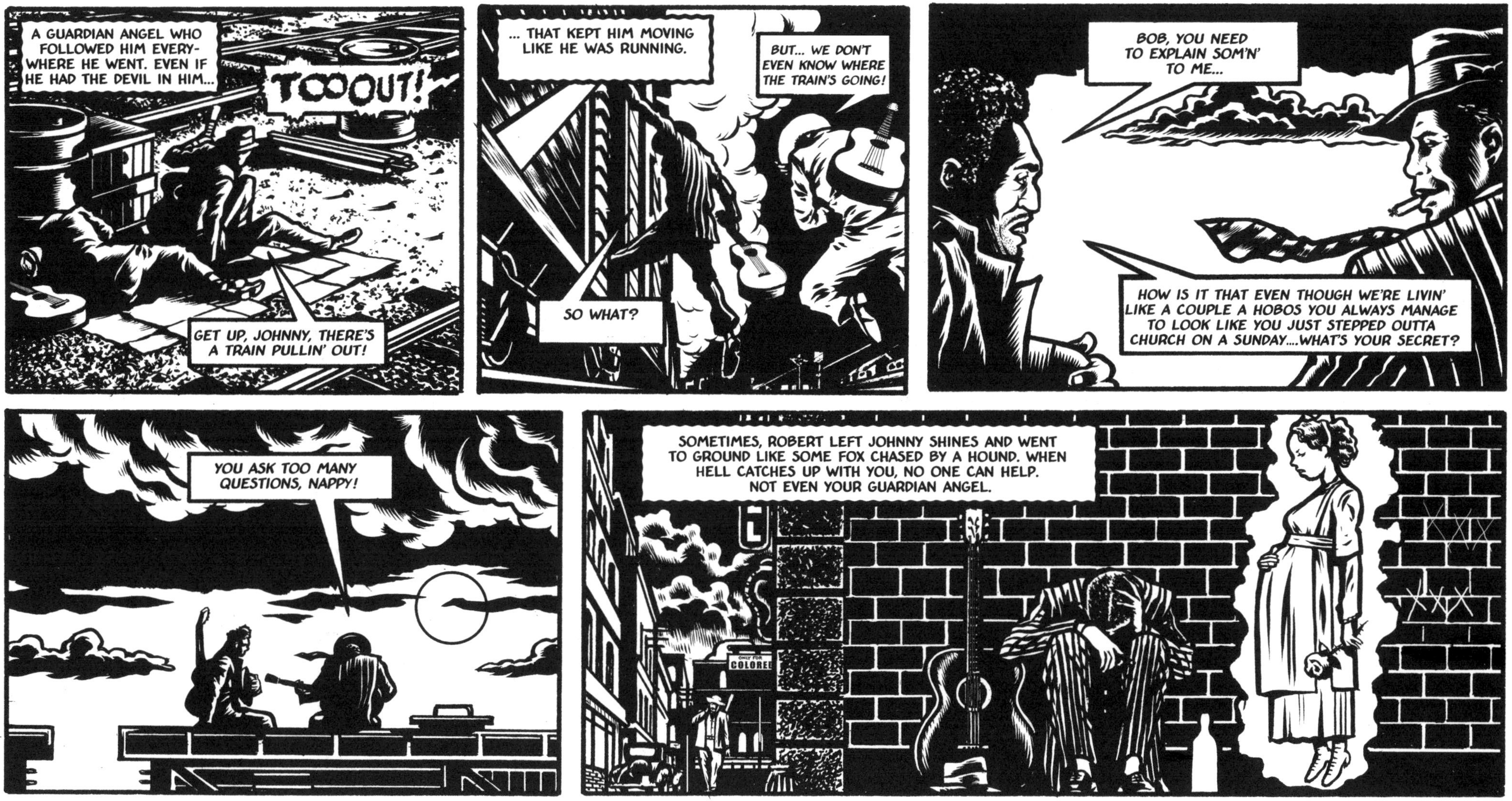
A GUARDIAN ANGEL WHO FOLLOWED HIM EVERY-WHERE HE WENT. EVEN IF HE HAD THE DEVIL IN HIM...
TOOOUT!
GET UP, JOHNNY, THERE'S A TRAIN PULLIN' OUT!
... THAT KEPT HIM MOVING LIKE HE WAS RUNNING.
BUT... WE DON'T EVEN KNOW WHERE THE TRAIN'S GOING!
SO WHAT?
BOB, YOU NEED TO EXPLAIN SOM'N' TO ME...
HOW IS IT THAT EVEN THOUGH WE'RE LIVIN' LIKE A COUPLE A HOBOS YOU ALWAYS MANAGE TO LOOK LIKE YOU JUST STEPPED OUTTA CHURCH ON A SUNDAY....WHAT'S YOUR SECRET?
YOU ASK TOO MANY QUESTIONS, NAPPY!
SOMETIMES, ROBERT LEFT JOHNNY SHINES AND WENT TO GROUND LIKE SOME FOX CHASED BY A HOUND. WHEN HELL CATCHES UP WITH YOU, NO ONE CAN HELP. NOT EVEN YOUR GUARDIAN ANGEL.
ONLY FOR COLORED

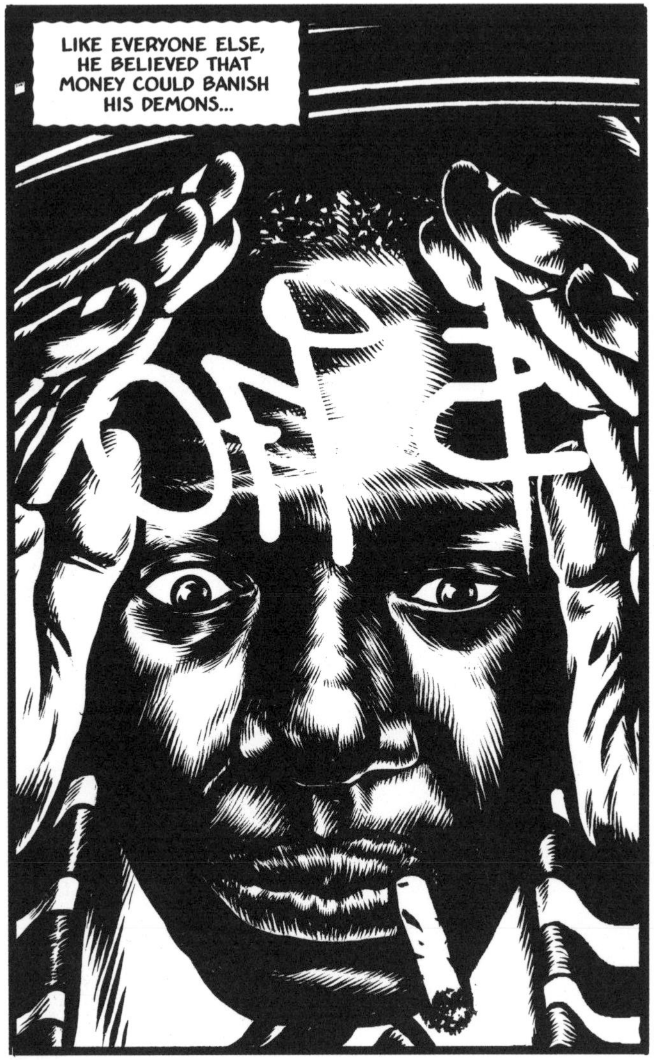
LIKE EVERYONE ELSE, HE BELIEVED THAT MONEY COULD BANISH HIS DEMONS...

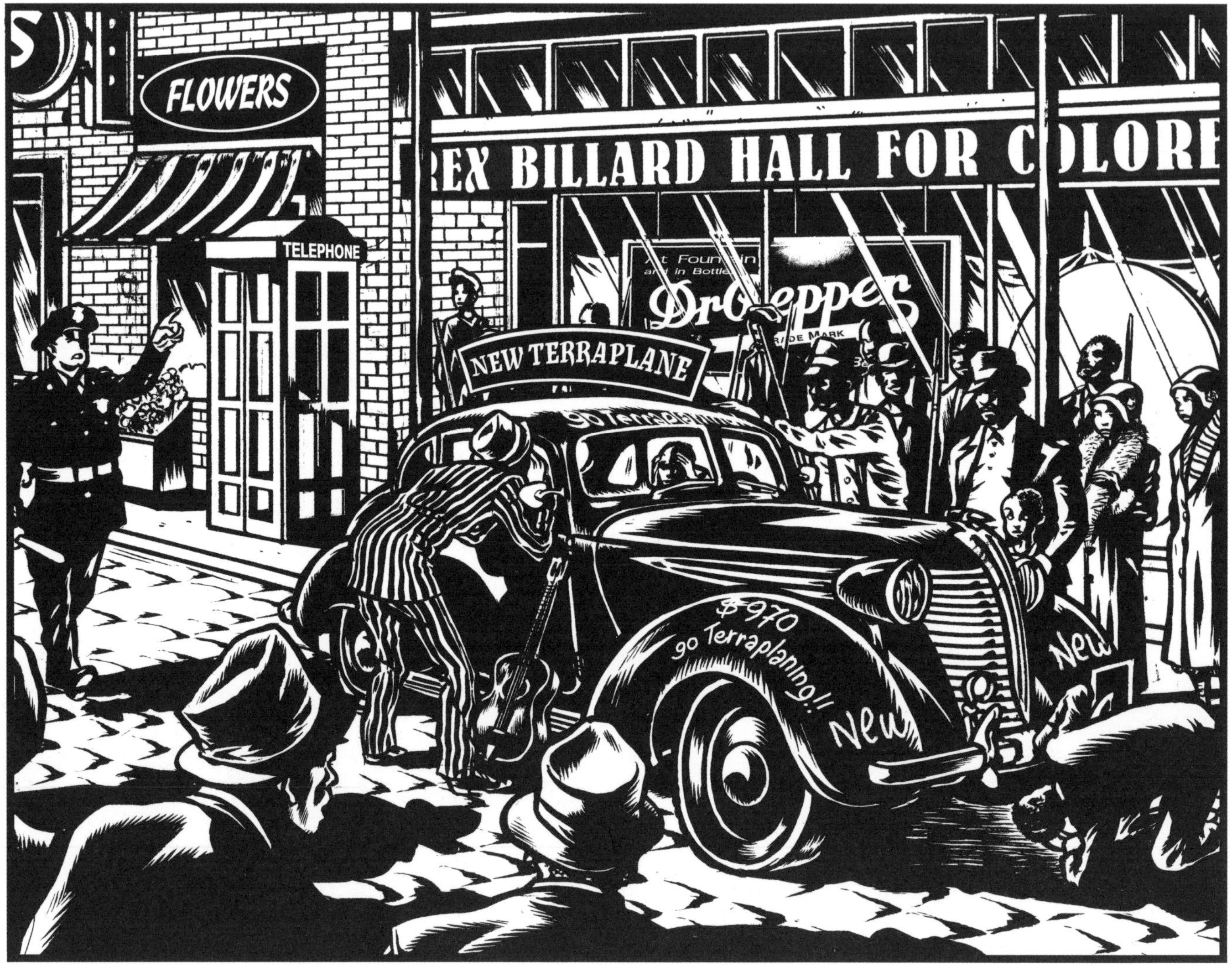
FLOWERS
TELEPHONE
REX BILLARD HALL FOR COLORE
NEW TERRAPLANE
$970
go Terraplaning!!
New
New

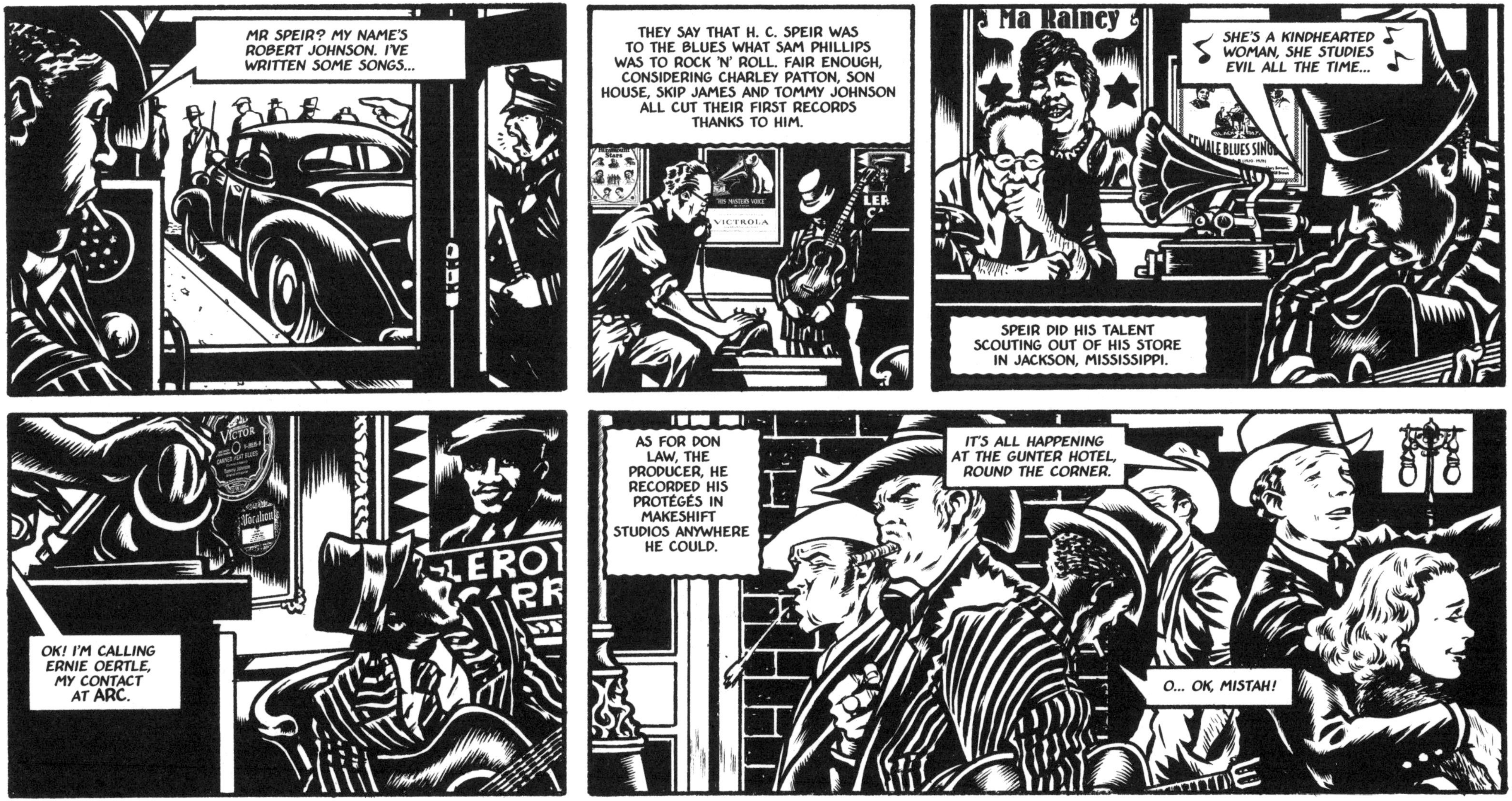
MR SPEIR? MY NAME'S ROBERT JOHNSON. I'VE WRITTEN SOME SONGS...
THEY SAY THAT H. C. SPEIR WAS TO THE BLUES WHAT SAM PHILLIPS WAS TO ROCK 'N' ROLL. FAIR ENOUGH, CONSIDERING CHARLEY PATTON, SON HOUSE, SKIP JAMES AND TOMMY JOHNSON ALL CUT THEIR FIRST RECORDS THANKS TO HIM.
"HIS MASTER'S VOICE"
VICTROLA
Ma Rainey
SHE'S A KINDHEARTED WOMAN, SHE STUDIES EVIL ALL THE TIME...
SPEIR DID HIS TALENT SCOUTING OUT OF HIS STORE IN JACKSON, MISSISSIPPI.
VICTOR
Vocalion
OK! I'M CALLING ERNIE OERTLE, MY CONTACT AT ARC.
AS FOR DON LAW, THE PRODUCER, HE RECORDED HIS PROTÉGÉS IN MAKESHIFT STUDIOS ANYWHERE HE COULD.
IT'S ALL HAPPENING AT THE GUNTER HOTEL, ROUND THE CORNER.
O... OK, MISTAH!

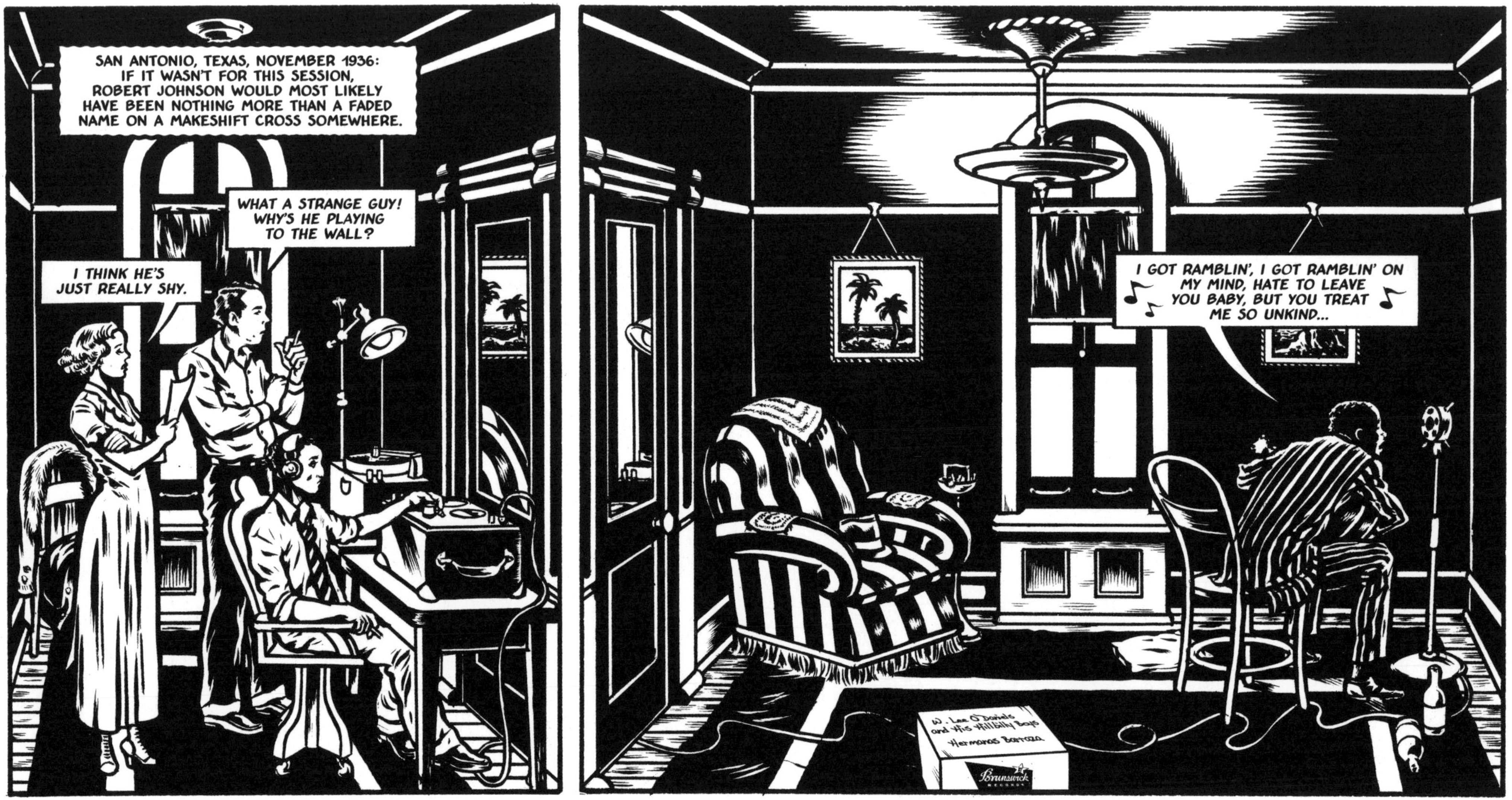
SAN ANTONIO, TEXAS, NOVEMBER 1936: IF IT WASN'T FOR THIS SESSION, ROBERT JOHNSON WOULD MOST LIKELY HAVE BEEN NOTHING MORE THAN A FADED NAME ON A MAKESHIFT CROSS SOMEWHERE.
WHAT A STRANGE GUY! WHY'S HE PLAYING TO THE WALL?
I THINK HE'S JUST REALLY SHY.
I GOT RAMBLIN', I GOT RAMBLIN' ON MY MIND, HATE TO LEAVE YOU BABY, BUT YOU TREAT ME SO UNKIND...
W. Lee O'Daniels and His Hillbilly Boys
Hermanos Barraza
Brunswick

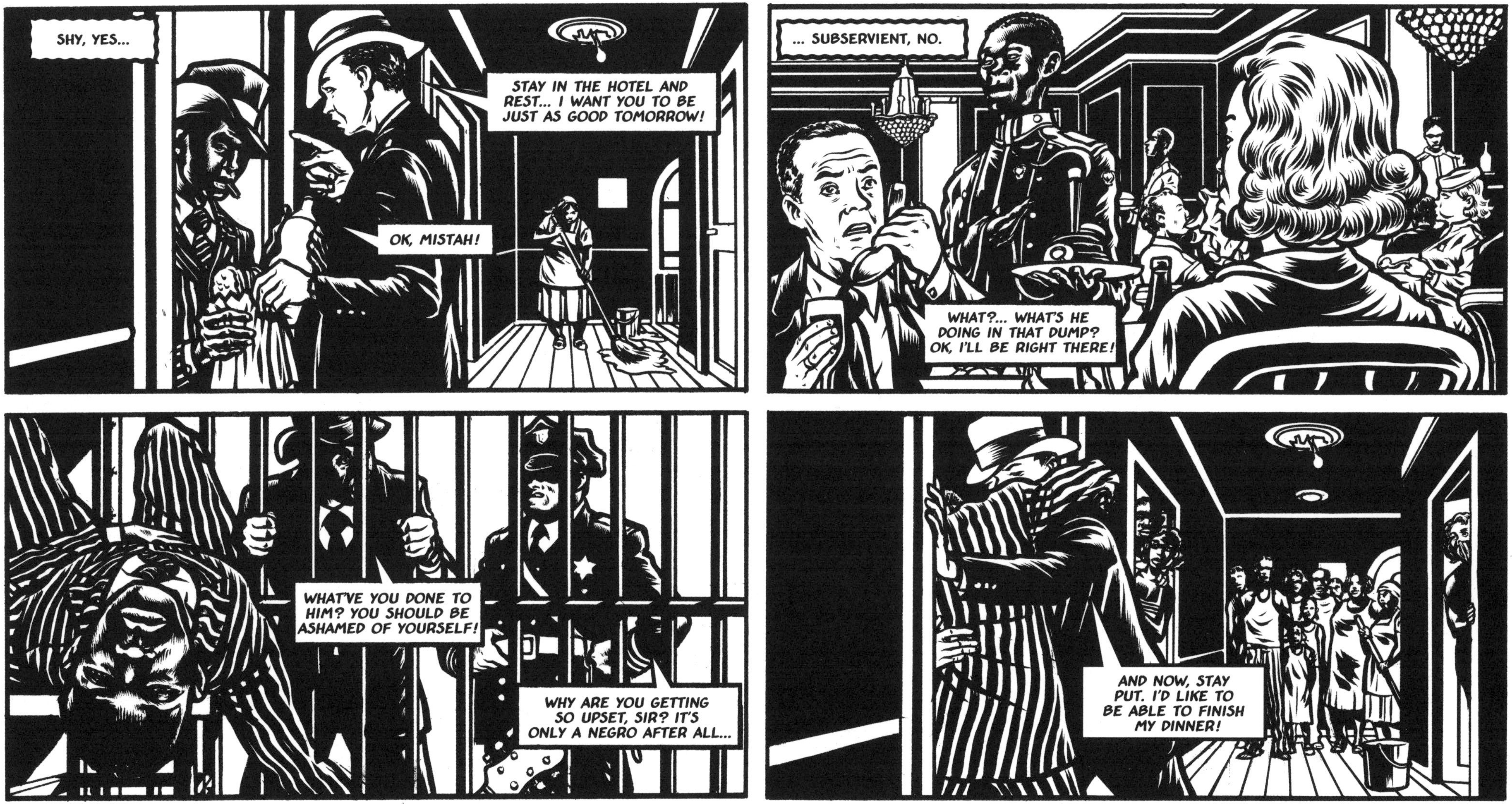
SHY, YES...
STAY IN THE HOTEL AND REST... I WANT YOU TO BE JUST AS GOOD TOMORROW!
OK, MISTAH!
... SUBSERVIENT, NO.
WHAT?... WHAT'S HE DOING IN THAT DUMP? OK, I'LL BE RIGHT THERE!
WHAT'VE YOU DONE TO HIM? YOU SHOULD BE ASHAMED OF YOURSELF!
WHY ARE YOU GETTING SO UPSET, SIR? IT'S ONLY A NEGRO AFTER ALL...
AND NOW, STAY PUT. I'D LIKE TO BE ABLE TO FINISH MY DINNER!

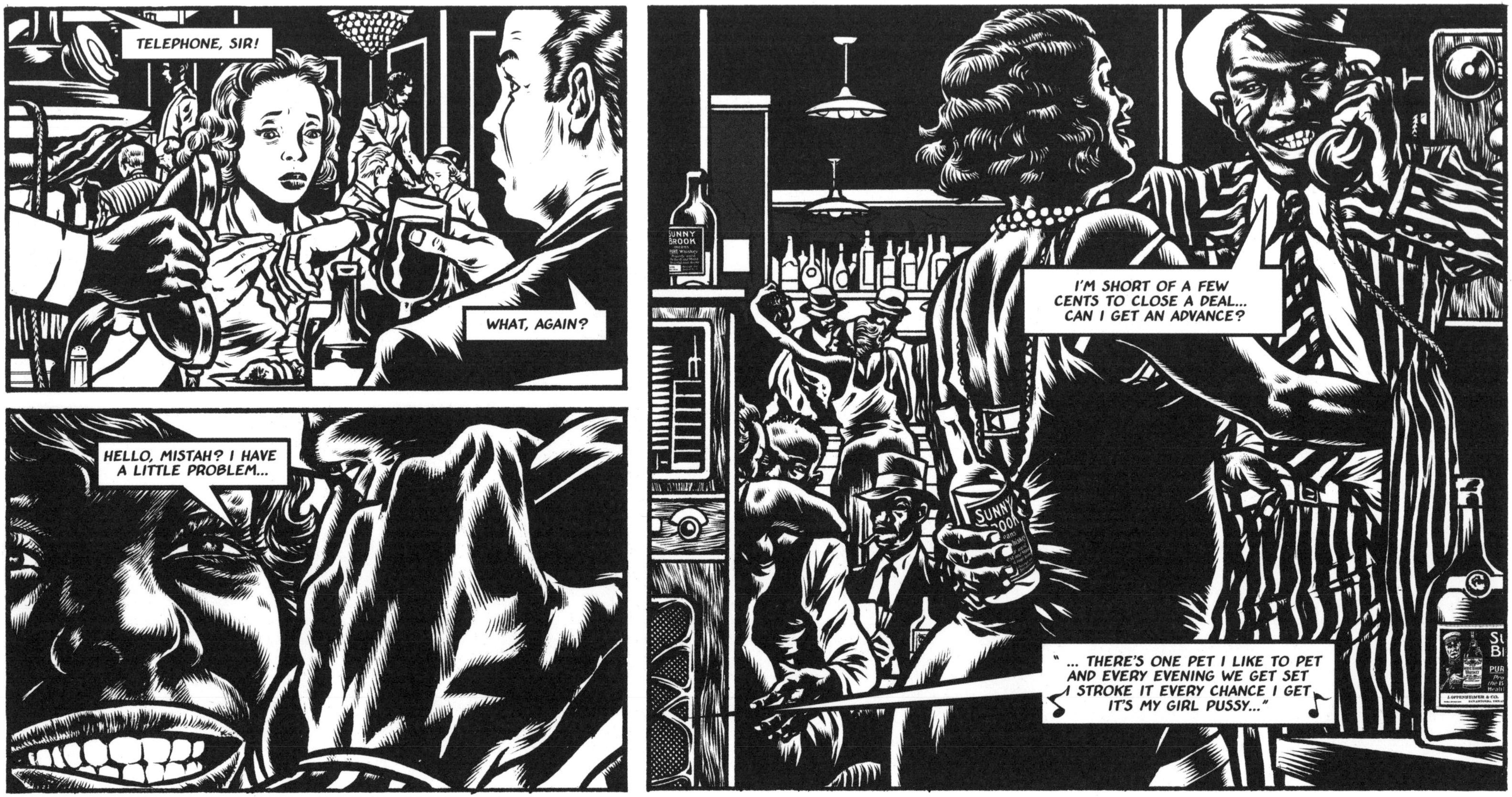
TELEPHONE, SIR!
WHAT, AGAIN?
HELLO, MISTAH? I HAVE A LITTLE PROBLEM...
I'M SHORT OF A FEW CENTS TO CLOSE A DEAL... CAN I GET AN ADVANCE?
" ... THERE'S ONE PET I LIKE TO PET
AND EVERY EVENING WE GET SET
I STROKE IT EVERY CHANCE I GET
IT'S MY GIRL PUSSY..."

Vocalion

Net tremed for
Radio Broadcast
(SA 2586)

Vocal Blues
with
Guitar Acc.

TERRAPLANE BLUES
-Robert Johnson-
ROBERT JOHNSON

TERRA   03416

5000 COPIES: A HUGE HIT AND A REAL BOOST FOR RACE RECORDS! BUT THAT WAS IT. AFTER THAT NO OTHER TITLES TOOK OFF, EVEN AFTER A SECOND RECORDING SESSION IN JUNE 1937 IN A WAREHOUSE IN DALLAS.

NEVERTHELESS, ROBERT'S RECORDS HAD MADE HIS NAME. HE WAS RESPECTED BY HIS LISTENERS AND THE BETTER RECORD LABELS.

YOU'D BETTER COME ON IN MY KITCHEN, 'CAUSE, IT'S GOIN' TO BE RAININ' OUTDOORS...
OH, SHE'S GONE, I KNOW SHE WON'T COME BACK...

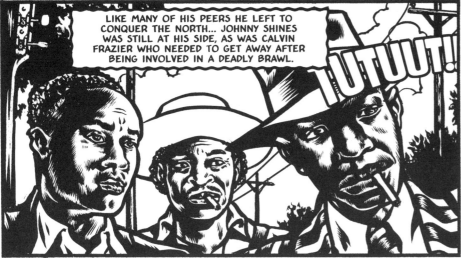

LIKE MANY OF HIS PEERS HE LEFT TO CONQUER THE NORTH... JOHNNY SHINES WAS STILL AT HIS SIDE, AS WAS CALVIN FRAZIER WHO NEEDED TO GET AWAY AFTER BEING INVOLVED IN A DEADLY BRAWL.

¡UTUUT!

OOH WILLIE MAE ALL MY LOVE'S IN VAIN...

WHO'S WILLIE MAE?

TENNESSEE

NORTH 51

POW! POW!

HONEYBOY EDWARDS' COUSIN.

TUUUUTT!

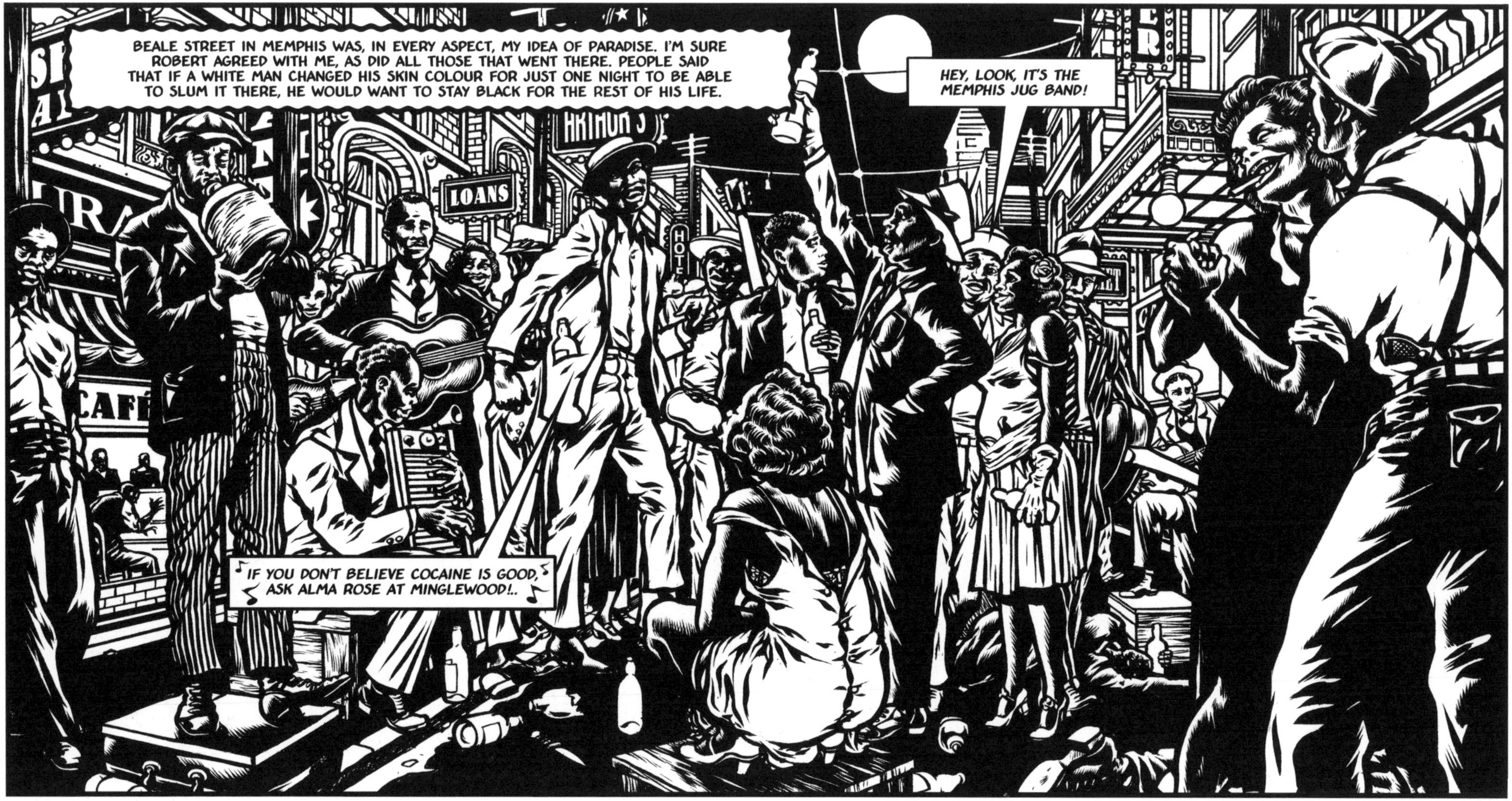
BEALE STREET IN MEMPHIS WAS, IN EVERY ASPECT, MY IDEA OF PARADISE. I'M SURE ROBERT AGREED WITH ME, AS DID ALL THOSE THAT WENT THERE. PEOPLE SAID THAT IF A WHITE MAN CHANGED HIS SKIN COLOUR FOR JUST ONE NIGHT TO BE ABLE TO SLUM IT THERE, HE WOULD WANT TO STAY BLACK FOR THE REST OF HIS LIFE.
HEY, LOOK, IT'S THE MEMPHIS JUG BAND!
LOANS
HOTEL
CAFÉ
IF YOU DON'T BELIEVE COCAINE IS GOOD, ASK ALMA ROSE AT MINGLEWOOD!..

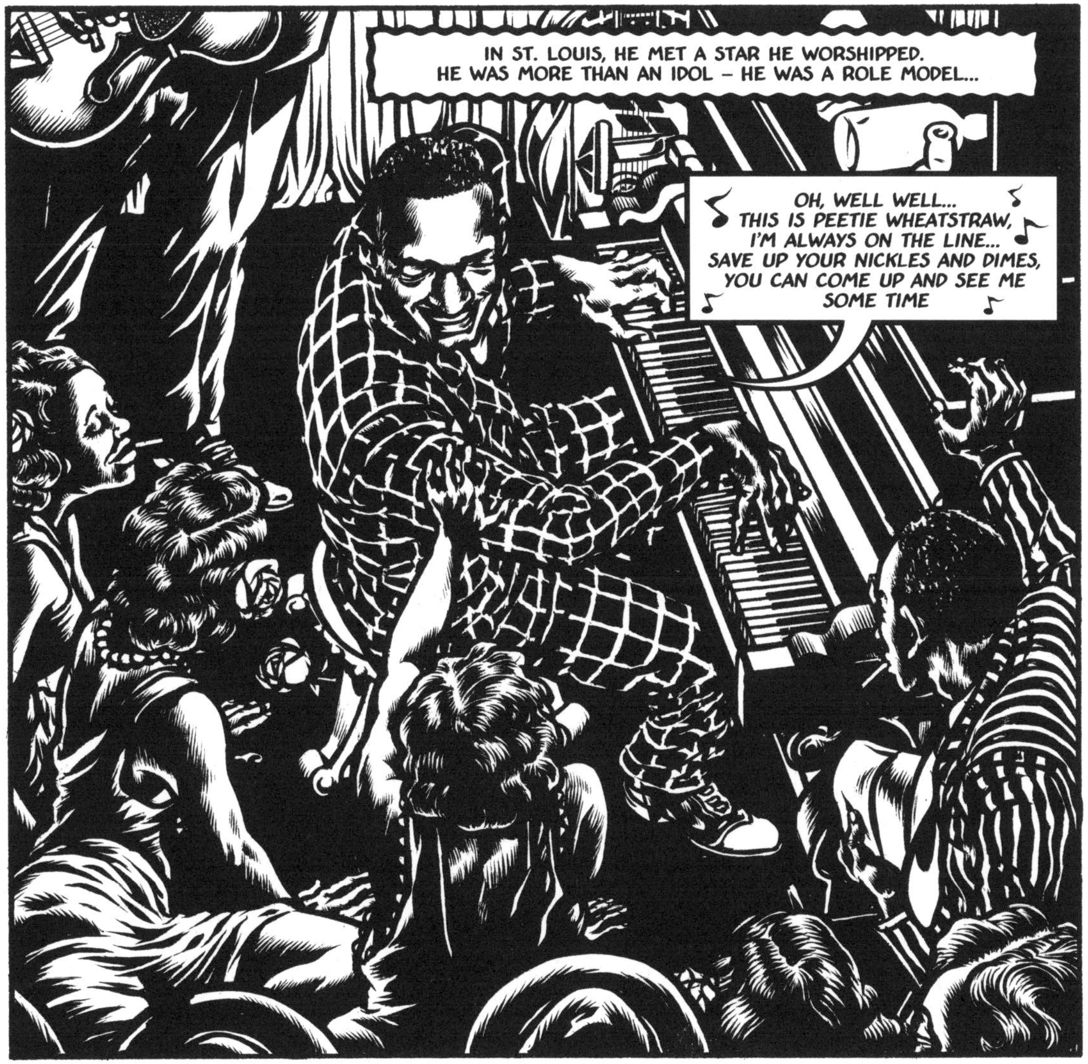
IN ST. LOUIS, HE MET A STAR HE WORSHIPPED. HE WAS MORE THAN AN IDOL – HE WAS A ROLE MODEL...
OH, WELL WELL... THIS IS PEETIE WHEATSTRAW, I'M ALWAYS ON THE LINE... SAVE UP YOUR NICKLES AND DIMES, YOU CAN COME UP AND SEE ME SOME TIME

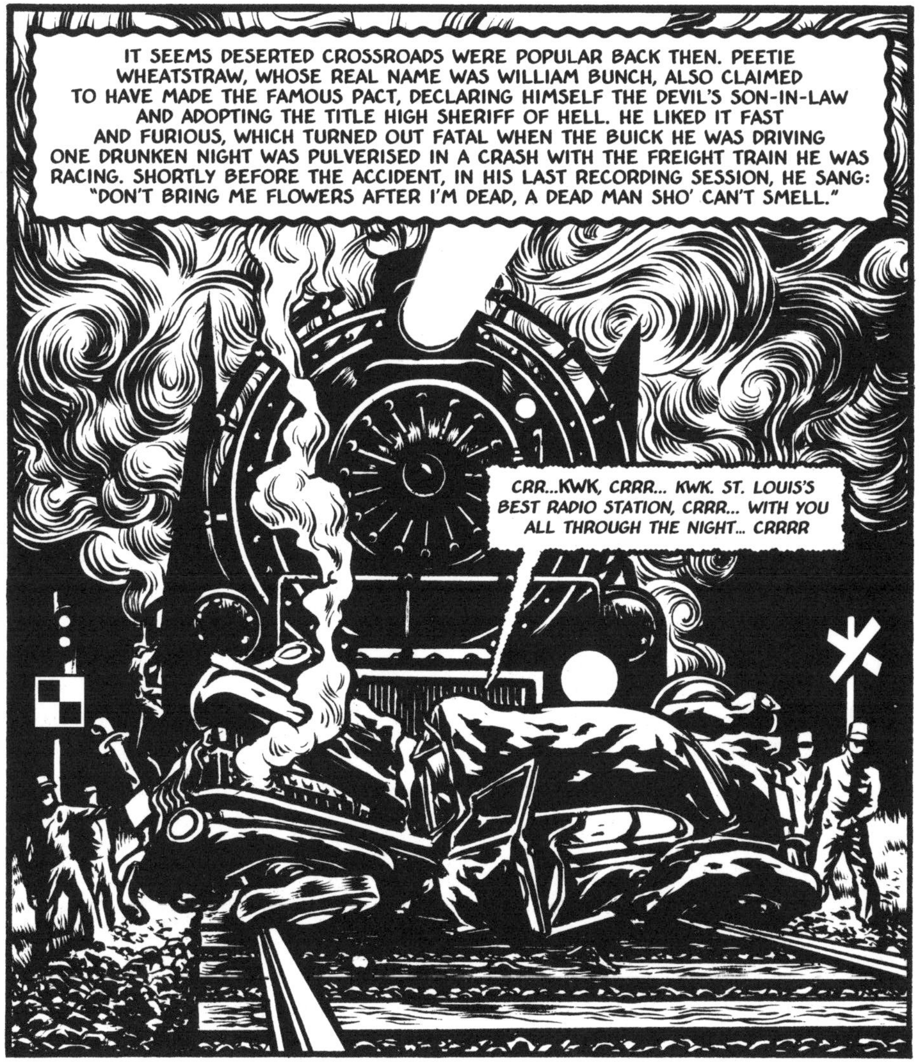
IT SEEMS DESERTED CROSSROADS WERE POPULAR BACK THEN. PEETIE WHEATSTRAW, WHOSE REAL NAME WAS WILLIAM BUNCH, ALSO CLAIMED TO HAVE MADE THE FAMOUS PACT, DECLARING HIMSELF THE DEVIL'S SON-IN-LAW AND ADOPTING THE TITLE HIGH SHERIFF OF HELL. HE LIKED IT FAST AND FURIOUS, WHICH TURNED OUT FATAL WHEN THE BUICK HE WAS DRIVING ONE DRUNKEN NIGHT WAS PULVERISED IN A CRASH WITH THE FREIGHT TRAIN HE WAS RACING. SHORTLY BEFORE THE ACCIDENT, IN HIS LAST RECORDING SESSION, HE SANG: "DON'T BRING ME FLOWERS AFTER I'M DEAD, A DEAD MAN SHO' CAN'T SMELL."
CRR...KWK, CRRR... KWK. ST. LOUIS'S BEST RADIO STATION, CRRR... WITH YOU ALL THROUGH THE NIGHT... CRRRR

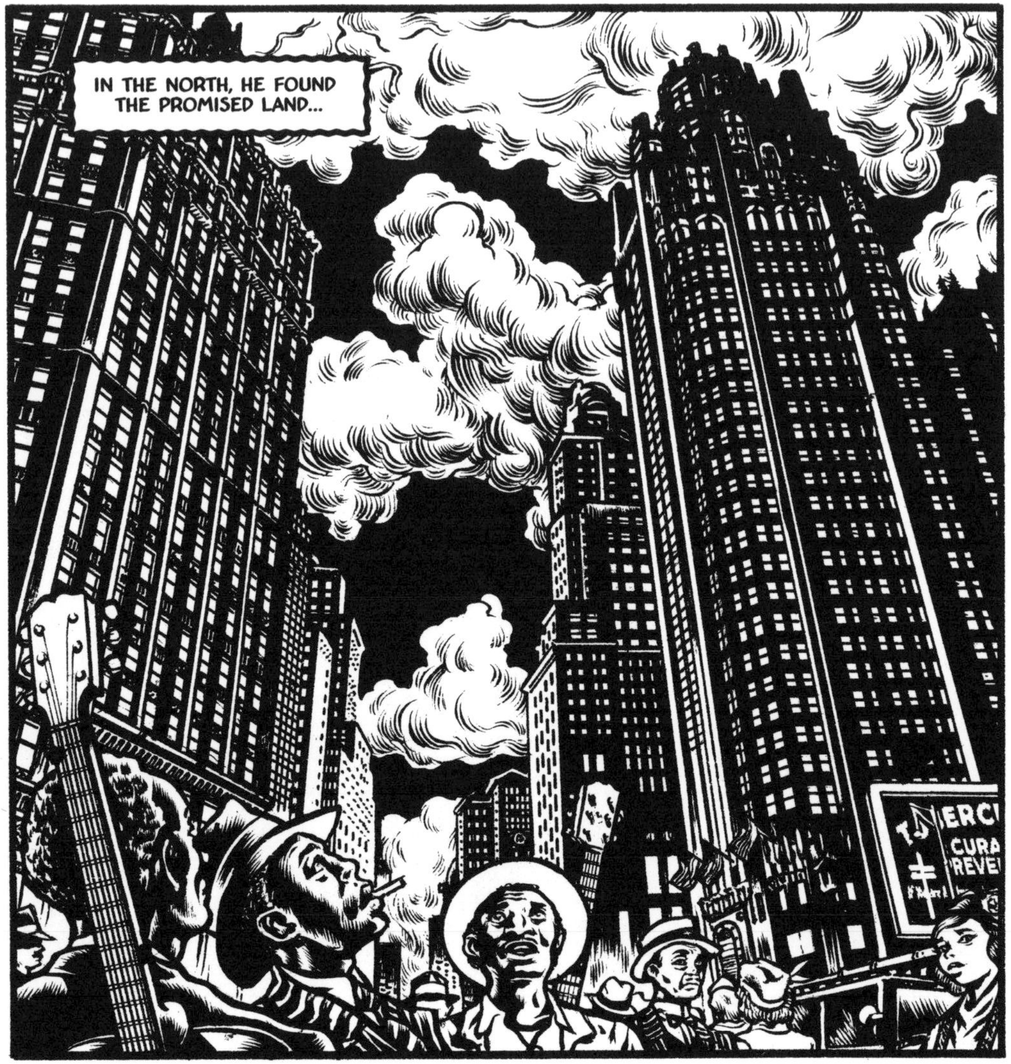
IN THE NORTH, HE FOUND THE PROMISED LAND...

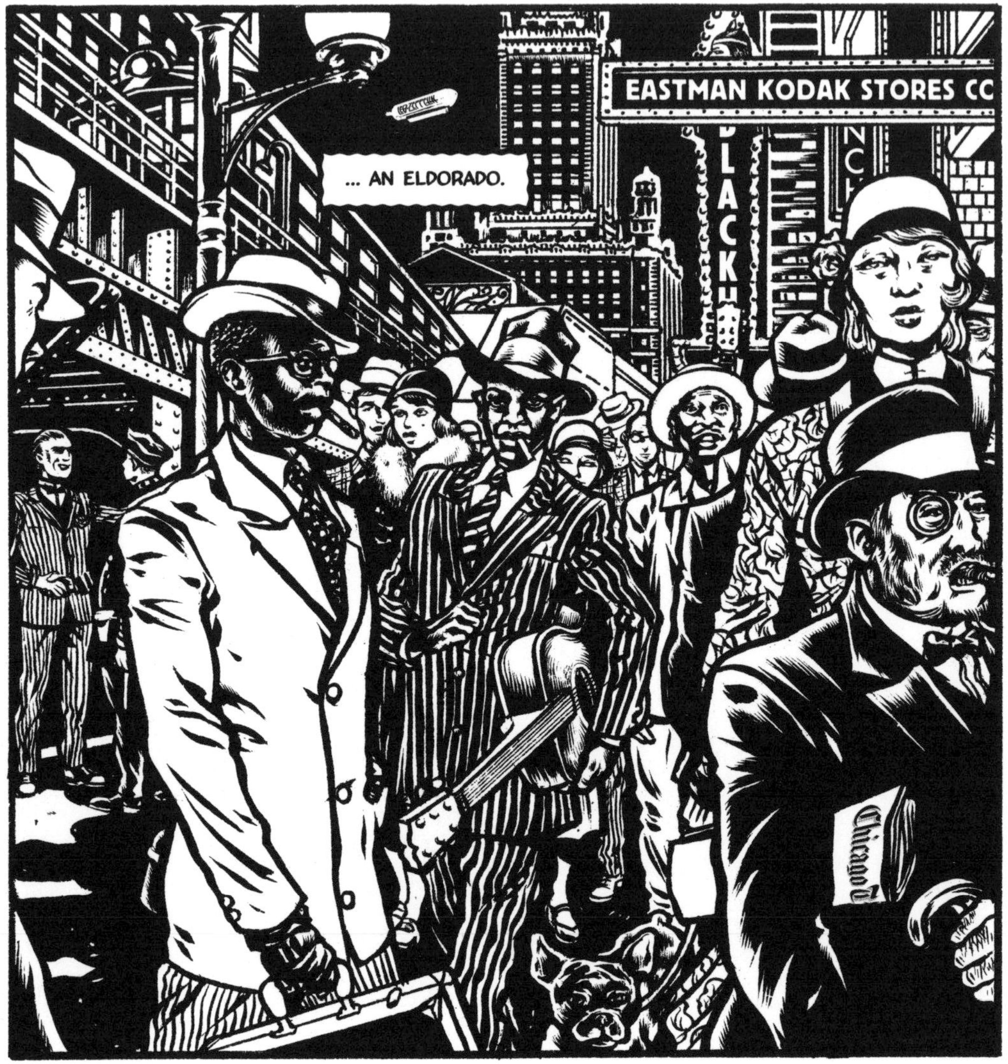
... AN ELDORADO.
EASTMAN KODAK STORES C

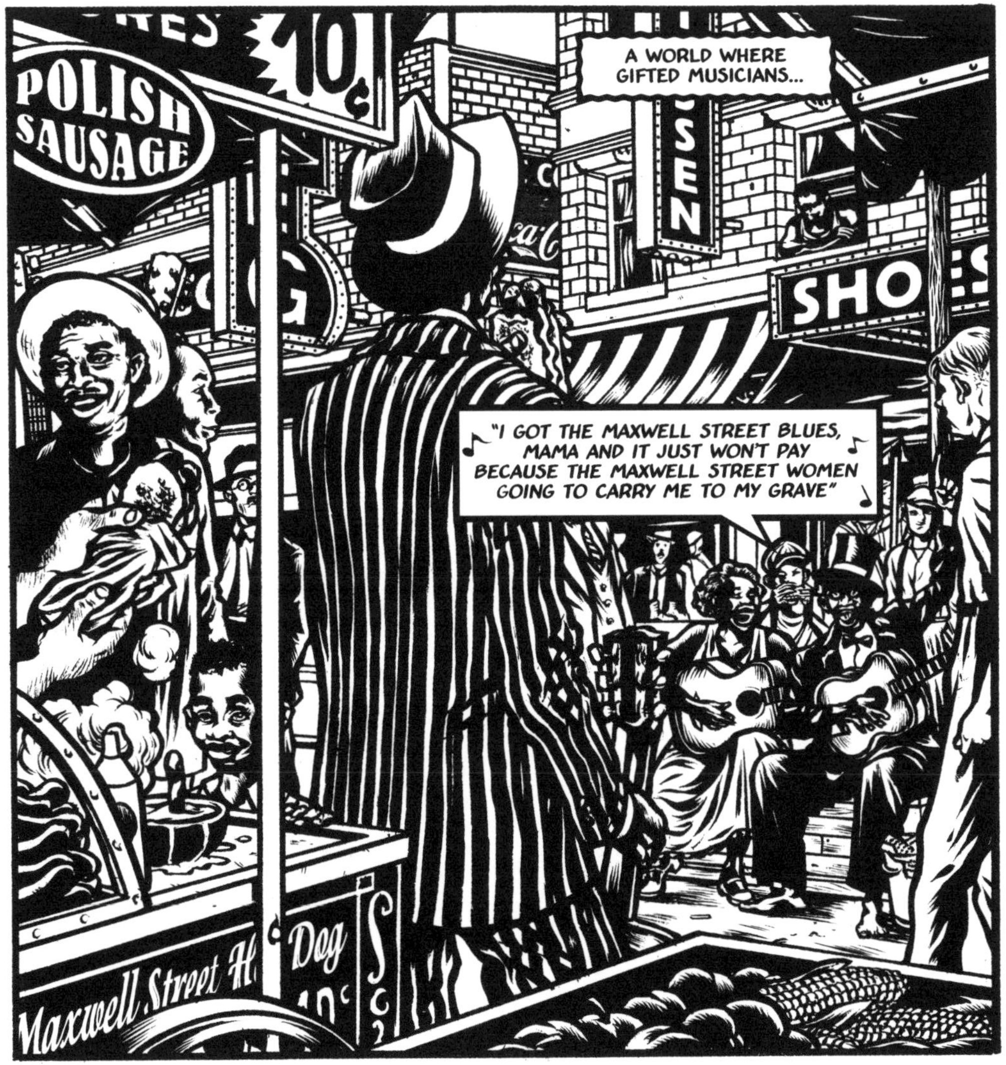
POLISH SAUSAGE
10¢
A WORLD WHERE GIFTED MUSICIANS...
"I GOT THE MAXWELL STREET BLUES, MAMA AND IT JUST WON'T PAY BECAUSE THE MAXWELL STREET WOMEN GOING TO CARRY ME TO MY GRAVE"

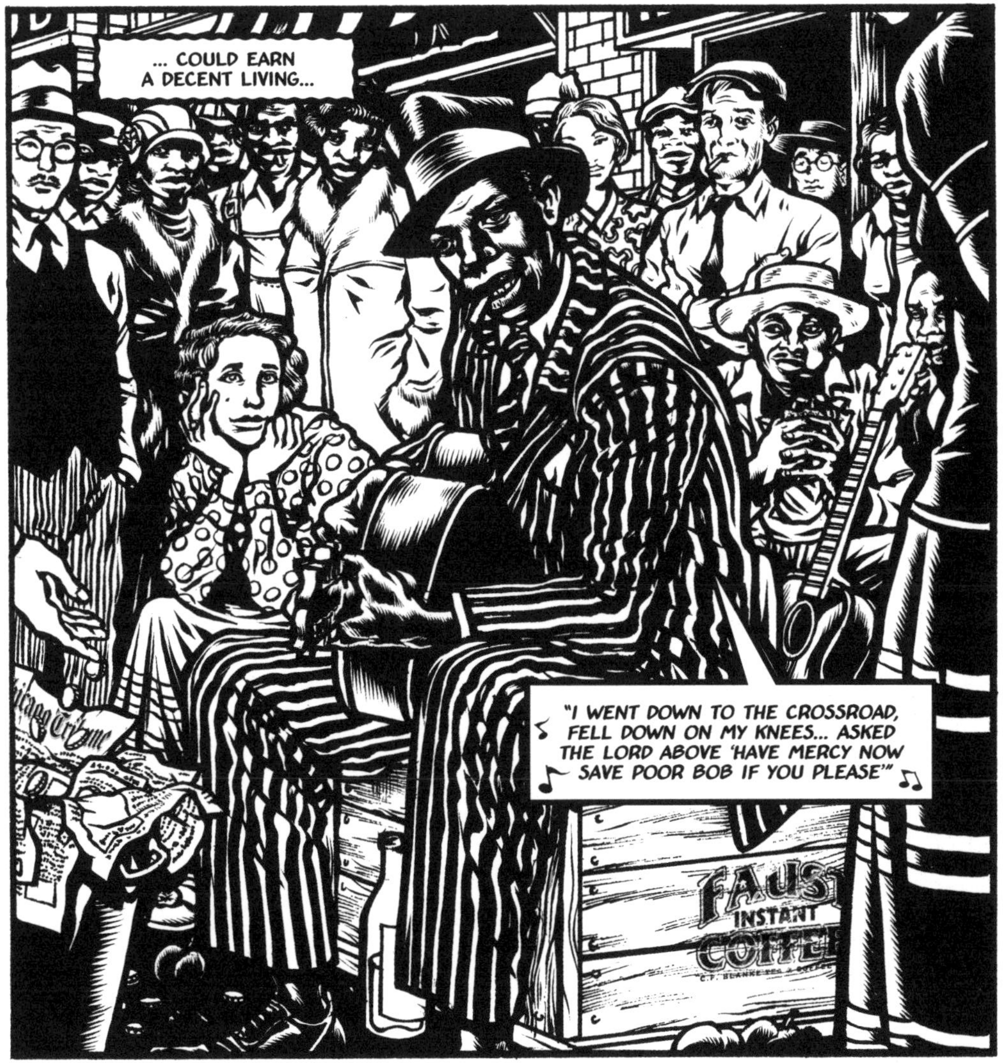
... COULD EARN A DECENT LIVING...
"I WENT DOWN TO THE CROSSROAD, FELL DOWN ON MY KNEES... ASKED THE LORD ABOVE 'HAVE MERCY NOW SAVE POOR BOB IF YOU PLEASE'"

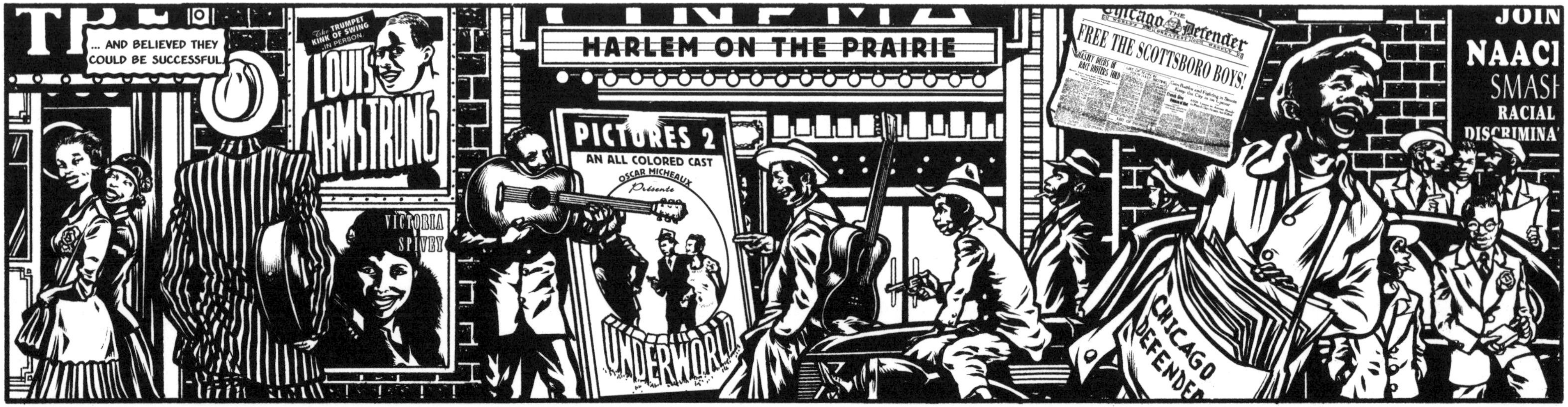
... AND BELIEVED THEY COULD BE SUCCESSFUL.
The TRUMPET KINK OF SWING IN PERSON
LOUIS ARMSTRONG
VICTORIA SPIVEY
HARLEM ON THE PRAIRIE
PICTURES 2
AN ALL COLORED CAST
OSCAR MICHEAUX
Présente
UNDERWORLD
FREE THE SCOTTSBORO BOYS!
CHICAGO DEFENDER
RACIAL

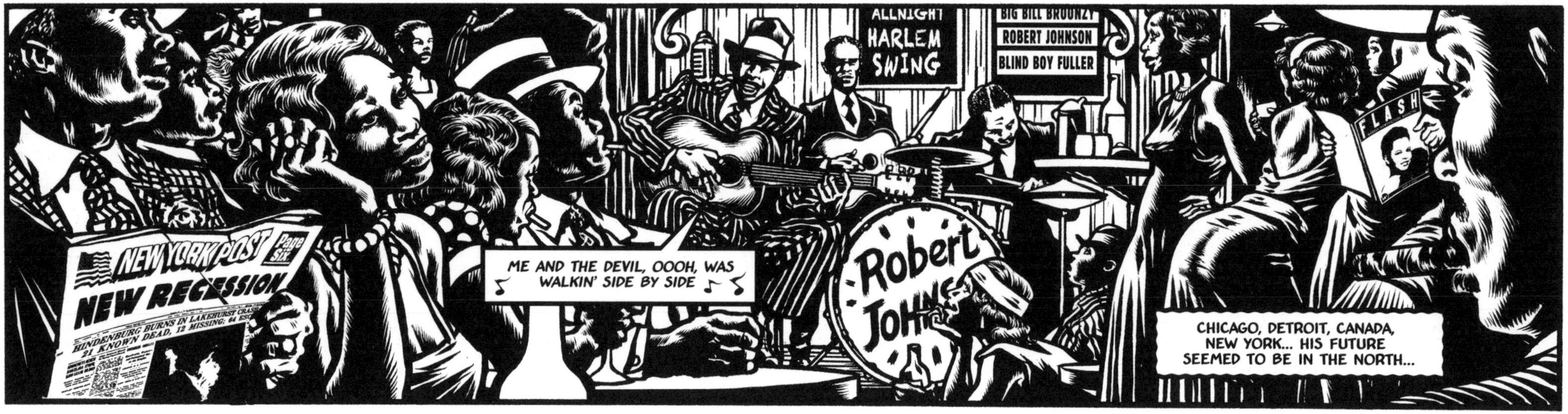
NEW YORK POST
Page Six
NEW RECESSION
ALLNIGHT HARLEM SWING
ROBERT JOHNSON
BLIND BOY FULLER
ME AND THE DEVIL, OOOH, WAS WALKIN' SIDE BY SIDE
Robert
FLASH
CHICAGO, DETROIT, CANADA, NEW YORK... HIS FUTURE SEEMED TO BE IN THE NORTH...

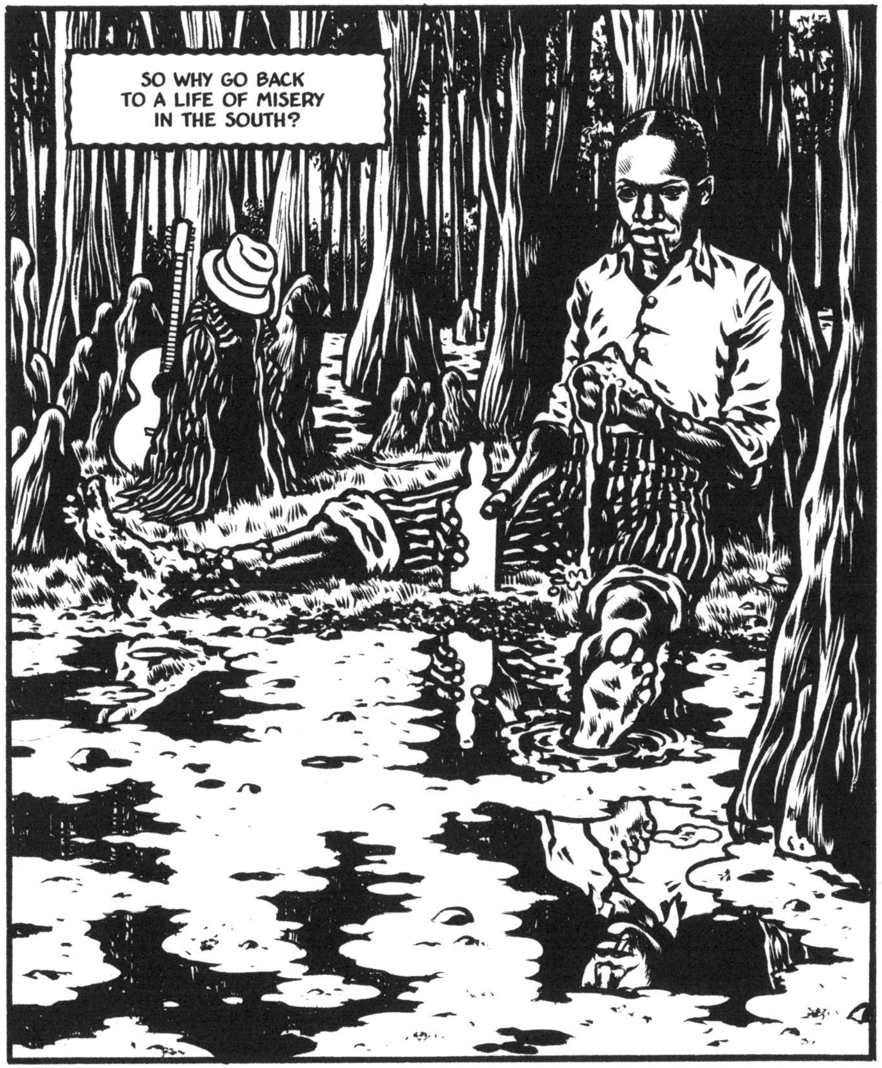
SO WHY GO BACK
TO A LIFE OF MISERY
IN THE SOUTH?

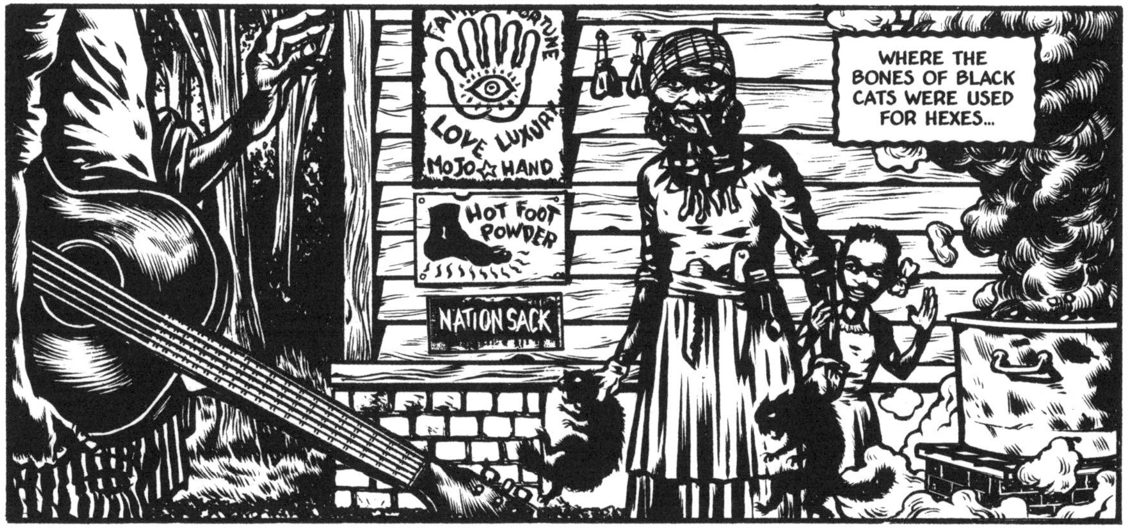
LOVE
MOJO HAND
HOT FOOT
POWDER
NATION SACK
WHERE THE
BONES OF BLACK
CATS WERE USED
FOR HEXES...

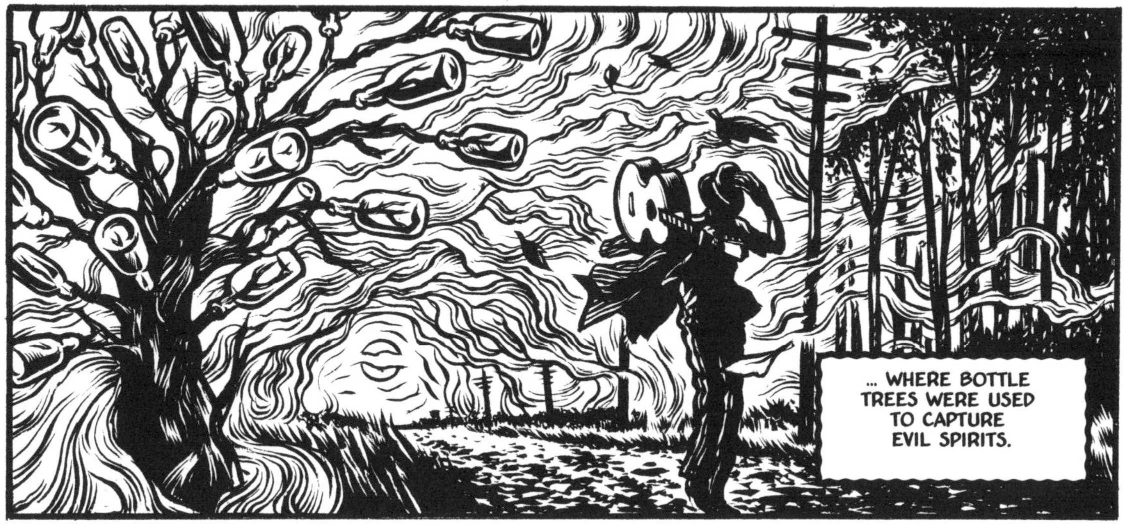
... WHERE BOTTLE
TREES WERE USED
TO CAPTURE
EVIL SPIRITS.

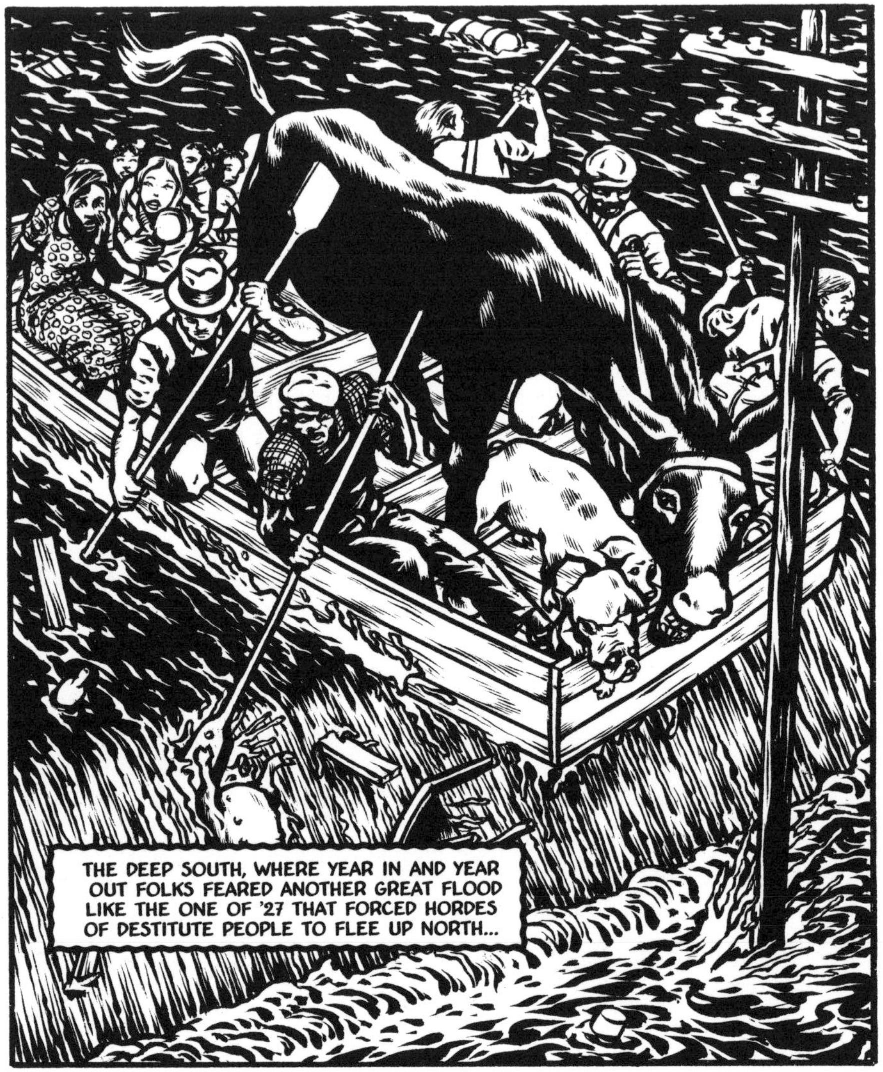
THE DEEP SOUTH, WHERE YEAR IN AND YEAR OUT FOLKS FEARED ANOTHER GREAT FLOOD LIKE THE ONE OF '27 THAT FORCED HORDES OF DESTITUTE PEOPLE TO FLEE UP NORTH...

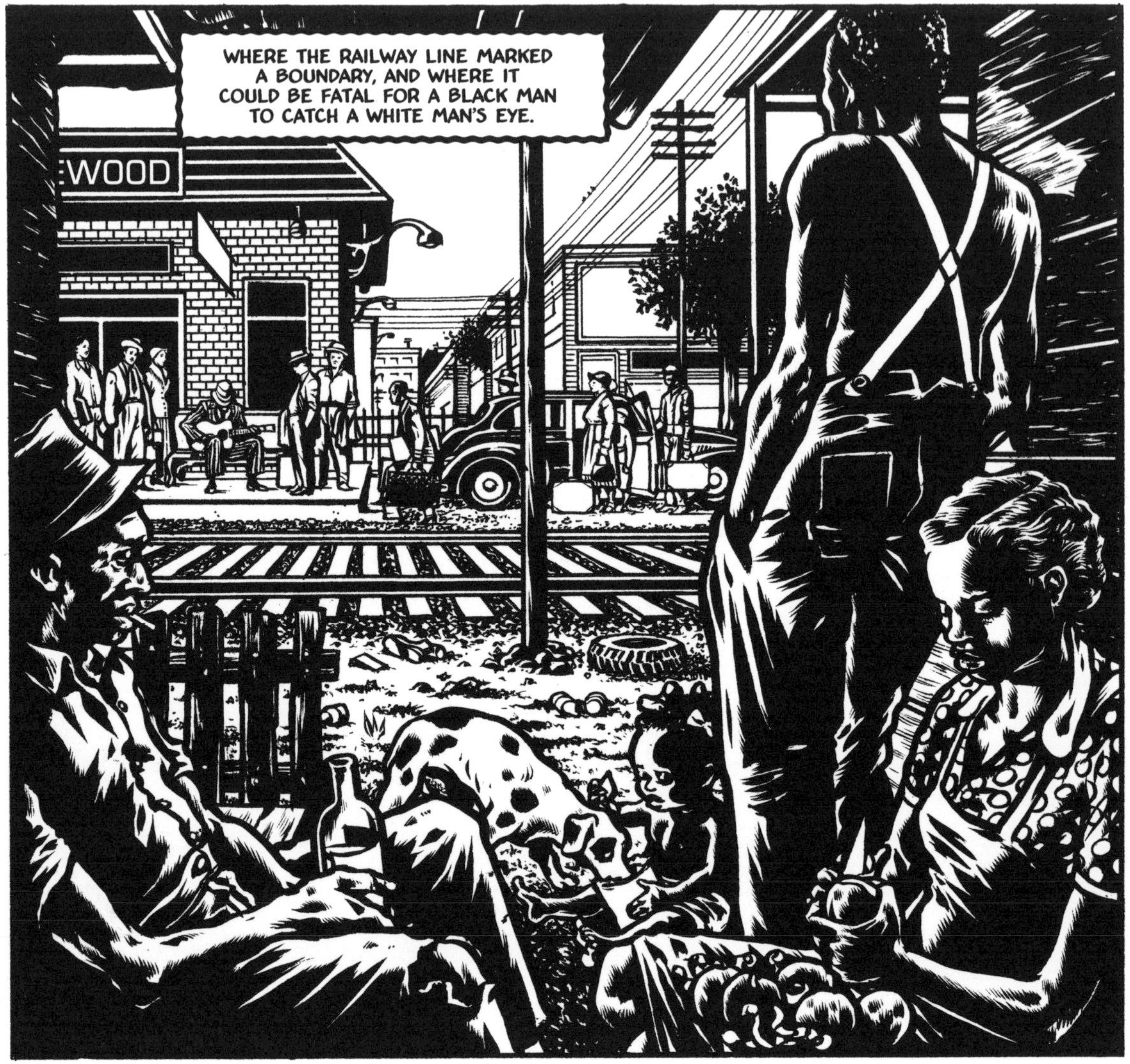
WHERE THE RAILWAY LINE MARKED A BOUNDARY, AND WHERE IT COULD BE FATAL FOR A BLACK MAN TO CATCH A WHITE MAN'S EYE.
WOOD

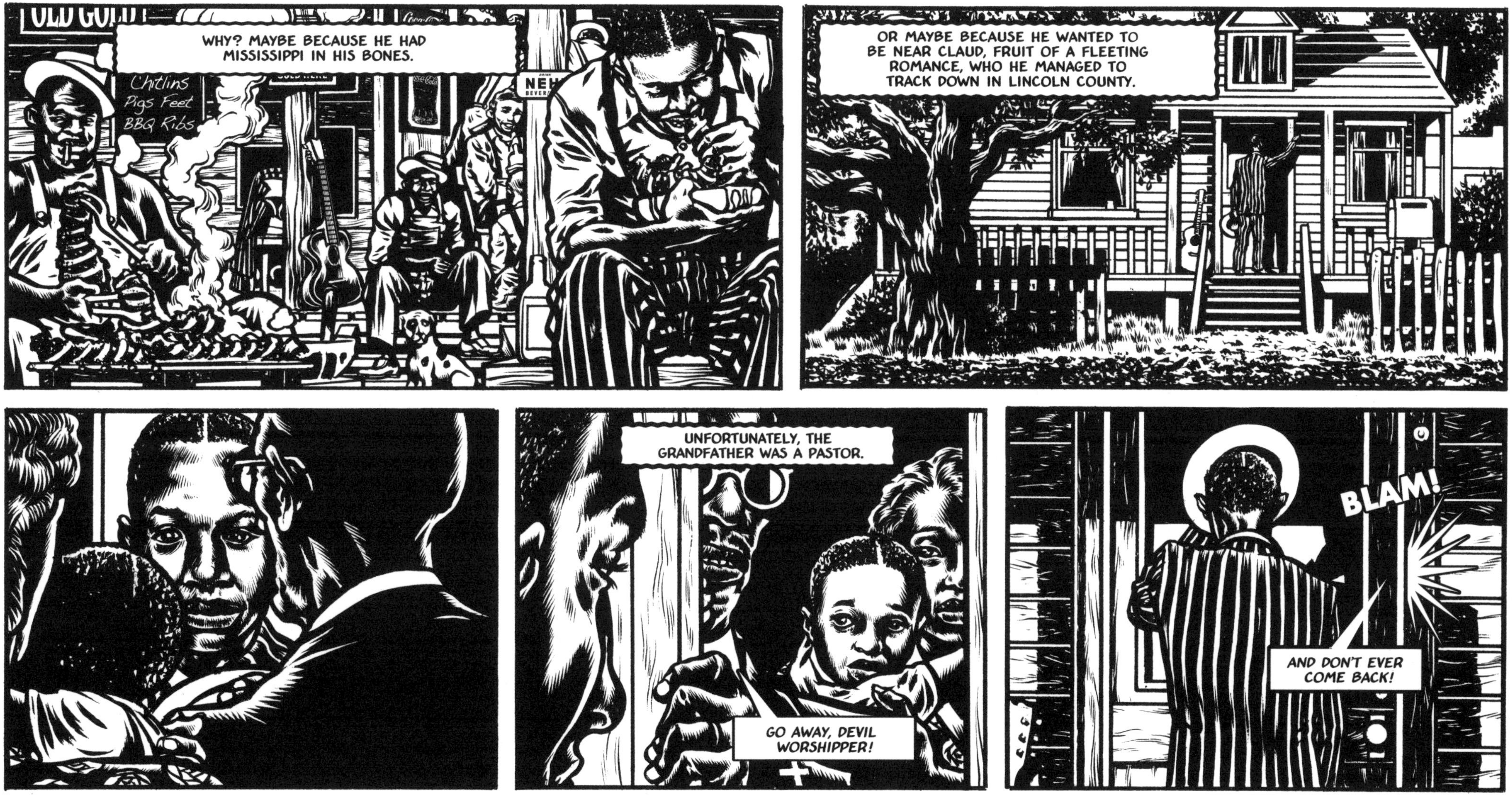
WHY? MAYBE BECAUSE HE HAD MISSISSIPPI IN HIS BONES.
Chitlins
Pigs Feet
BBQ Ribs
OR MAYBE BECAUSE HE WANTED TO BE NEAR CLAUD, FRUIT OF A FLEETING ROMANCE, WHO HE MANAGED TO TRACK DOWN IN LINCOLN COUNTY.
UNFORTUNATELY, THE GRANDFATHER WAS A PASTOR.
GO AWAY, DEVIL WORSHIPPER!
BLAM!
AND DON'T EVER COME BACK!

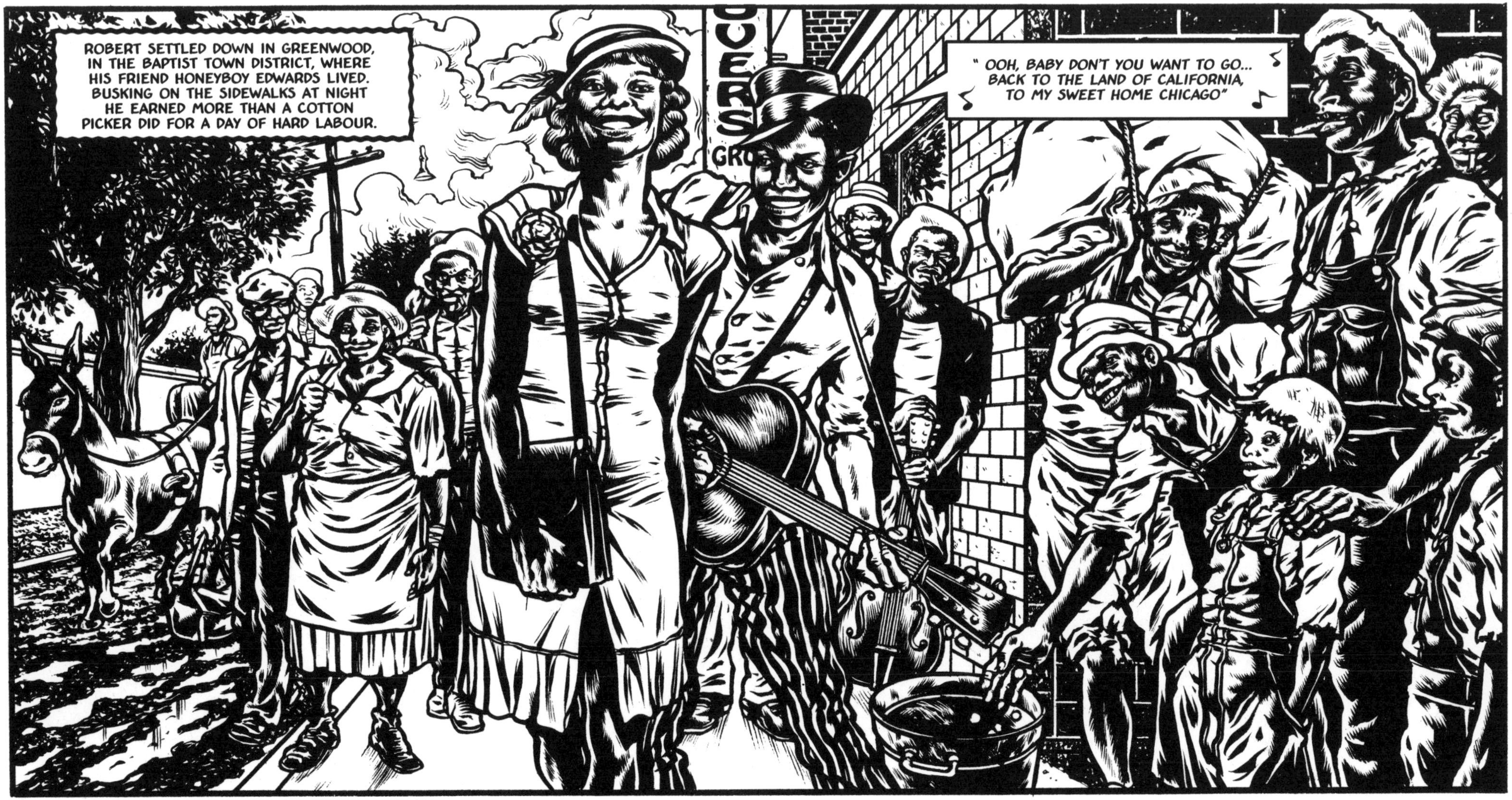
ROBERT SETTLED DOWN IN GREENWOOD, IN THE BAPTIST TOWN DISTRICT, WHERE HIS FRIEND HONEYBOY EDWARDS LIVED. BUSKING ON THE SIDEWALKS AT NIGHT HE EARNED MORE THAN A COTTON PICKER DID FOR A DAY OF HARD LABOUR.
" OOH, BABY DON'T YOU WANT TO GO... BACK TO THE LAND OF CALIFORNIA, TO MY SWEET HOME CHICAGO"

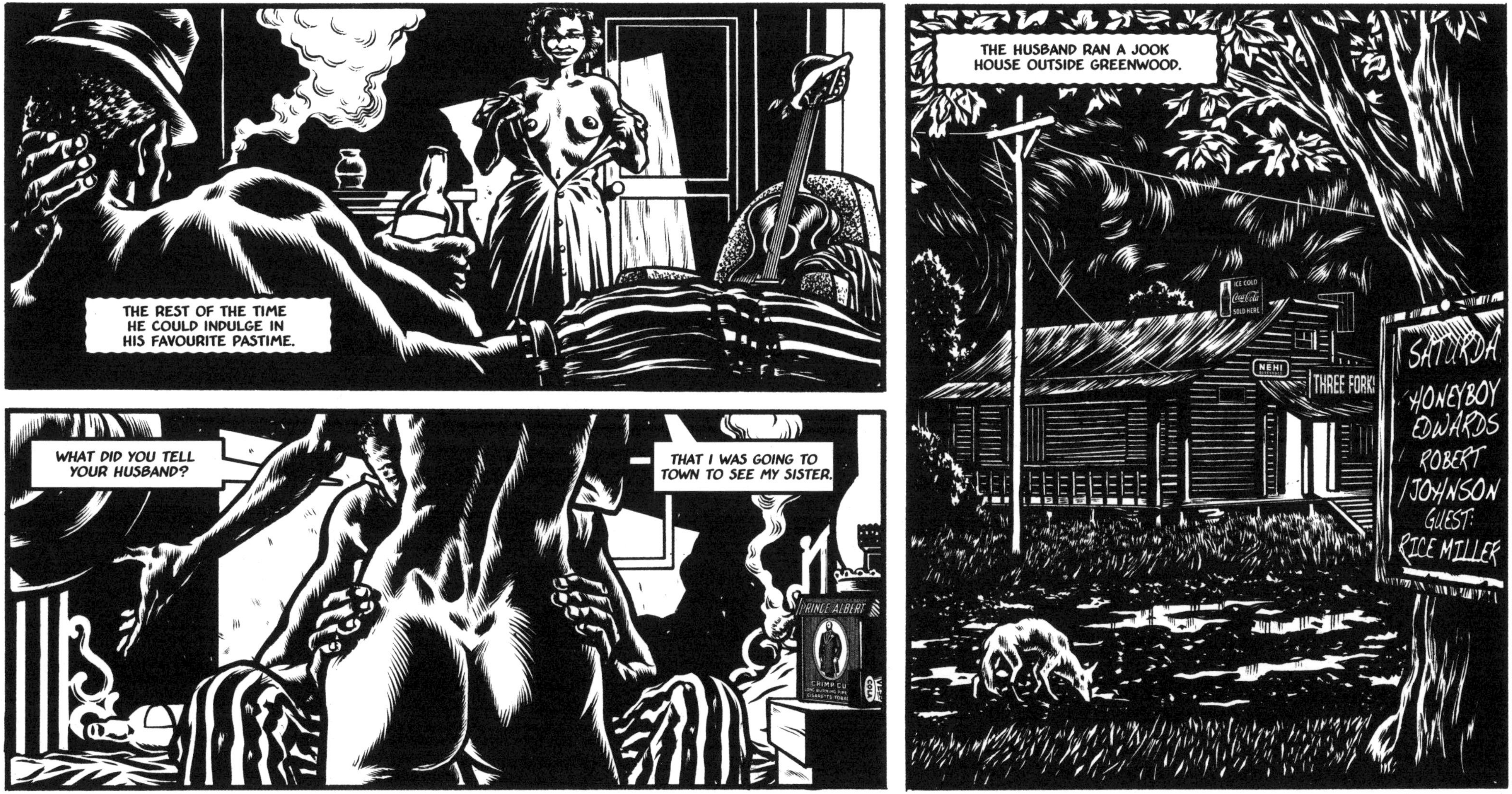
THE REST OF THE TIME HE COULD INDULGE IN HIS FAVOURITE PASTIME.
WHAT DID YOU TELL YOUR HUSBAND?
THAT I WAS GOING TO TOWN TO SEE MY SISTER.
PRINCE ALBERT
CRIMP CUT
THE HUSBAND RAN A JOOK HOUSE OUTSIDE GREENWOOD.
ICE COLD
Coca-Cola
SOLD HERE
NEHI
THREE FORKS
SATURDA
HONEYBOY EDWARDS
ROBERT JOHNSON
GUEST:
RICE MILLER

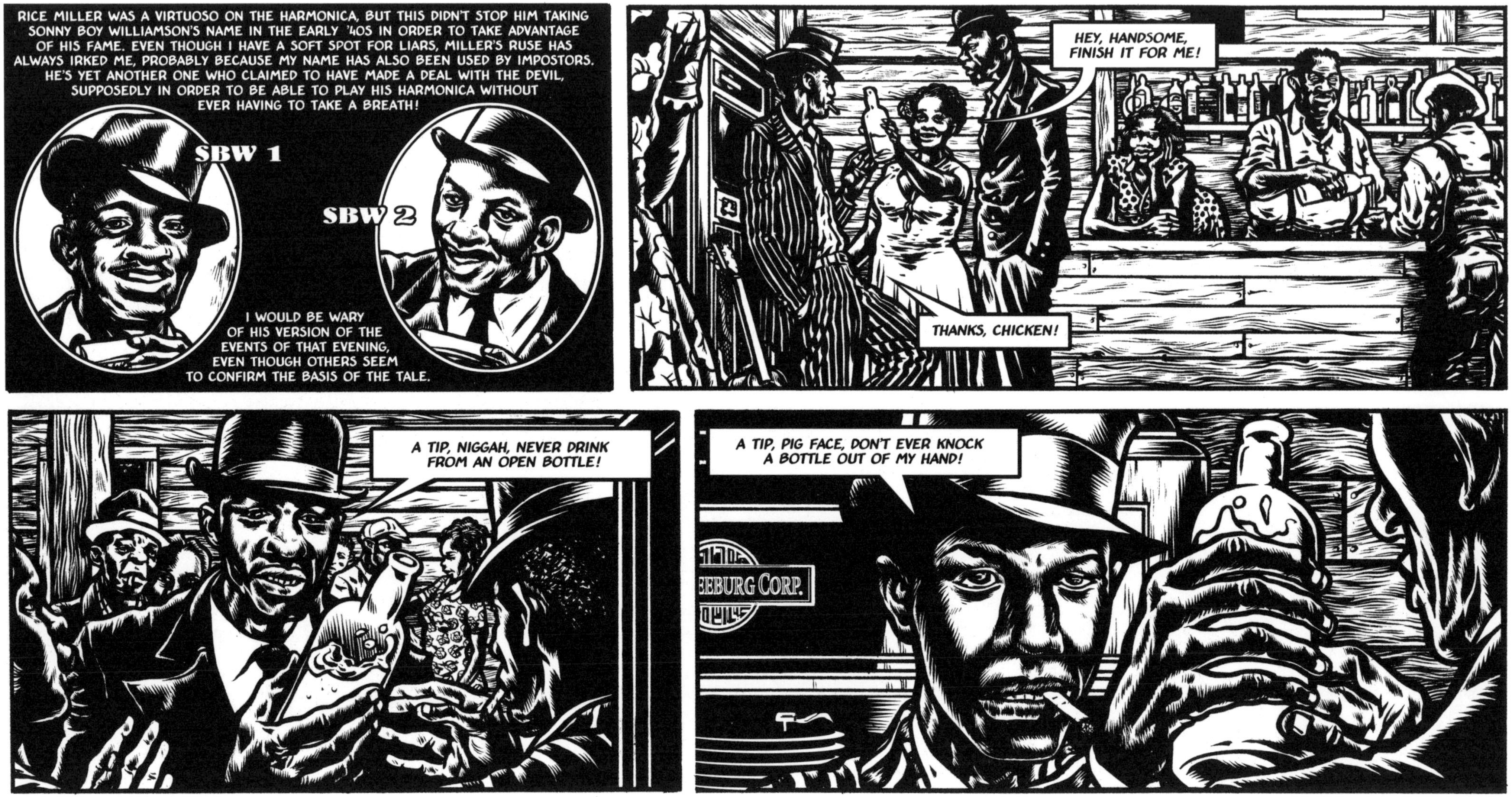

RICE MILLER WAS A VIRTUOSO ON THE HARMONICA, BUT THIS DIDN'T STOP HIM TAKING SONNY BOY WILLIAMSON'S NAME IN THE EARLY '40S IN ORDER TO TAKE ADVANTAGE OF HIS FAME. EVEN THOUGH I HAVE A SOFT SPOT FOR LIARS, MILLER'S RUSE HAS ALWAYS IRKED ME, PROBABLY BECAUSE MY NAME HAS ALSO BEEN USED BY IMPOSTORS. HE'S YET ANOTHER ONE WHO CLAIMED TO HAVE MADE A DEAL WITH THE DEVIL, SUPPOSEDLY IN ORDER TO BE ABLE TO PLAY HIS HARMONICA WITHOUT EVER HAVING TO TAKE A BREATH!
SBW 1
SBW 2
I WOULD BE WARY OF HIS VERSION OF THE EVENTS OF THAT EVENING, EVEN THOUGH OTHERS SEEM TO CONFIRM THE BASIS OF THE TALE.
HEY, HANDSOME, FINISH IT FOR ME!
THANKS, CHICKEN!
A TIP, NIGGAH, NEVER DRINK FROM AN OPEN BOTTLE!
A TIP, PIG FACE, DON'T EVER KNOCK A BOTTLE OUT OF MY HAND!
EEBURG CORP.

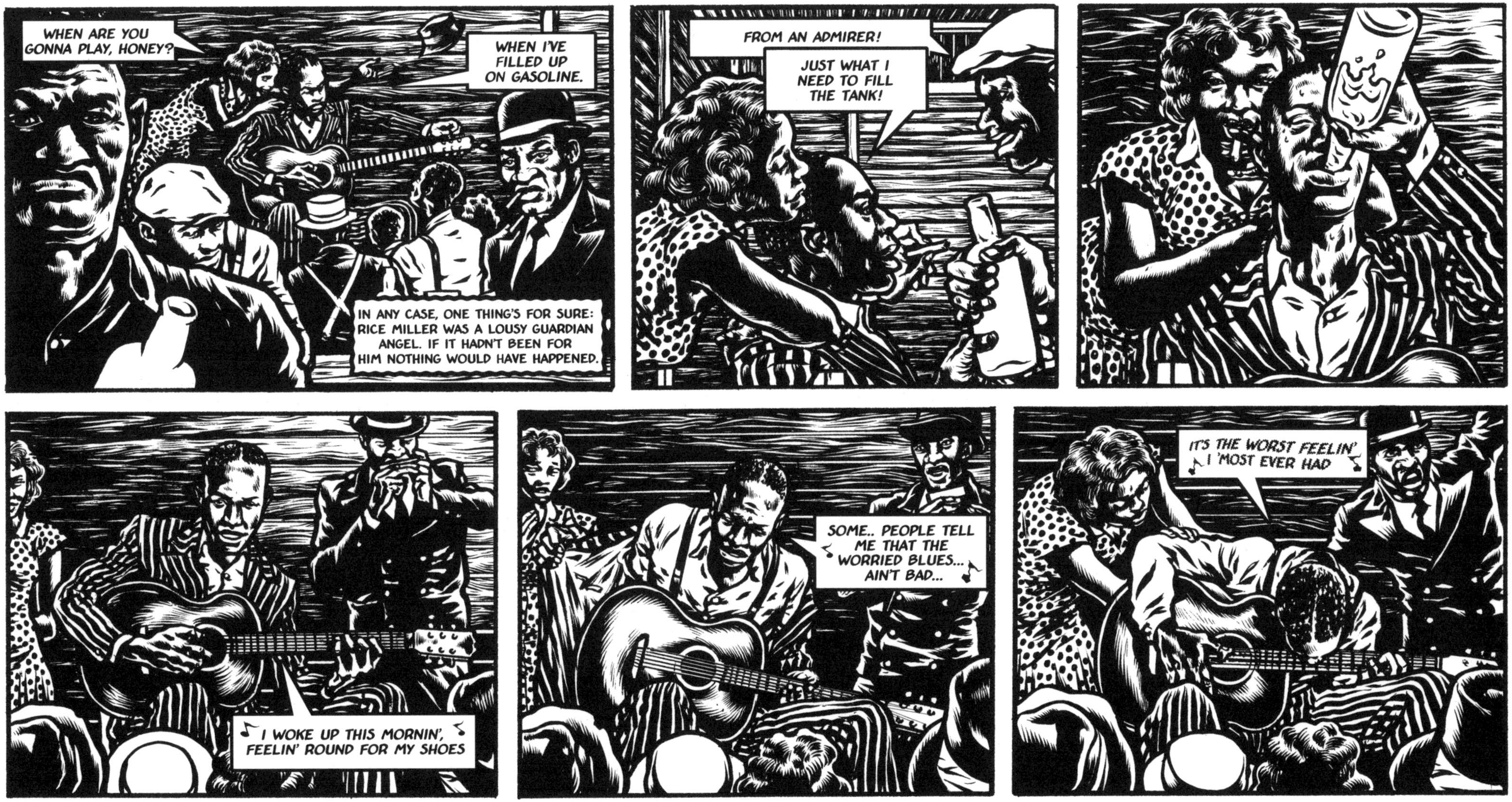
WHEN ARE YOU GONNA PLAY, HONEY?
WHEN I'VE FILLED UP ON GASOLINE.
IN ANY CASE, ONE THING'S FOR SURE: RICE MILLER WAS A LOUSY GUARDIAN ANGEL. IF IT HADN'T BEEN FOR HIM NOTHING WOULD HAVE HAPPENED.
FROM AN ADMIRER!
JUST WHAT I NEED TO FILL THE TANK!
I WOKE UP THIS MORNIN', FEELIN' ROUND FOR MY SHOES
SOME.. PEOPLE TELL ME THAT THE WORRIED BLUES... AIN'T BAD...
IT'S THE WORST FEELIN' I 'MOST EVER HAD

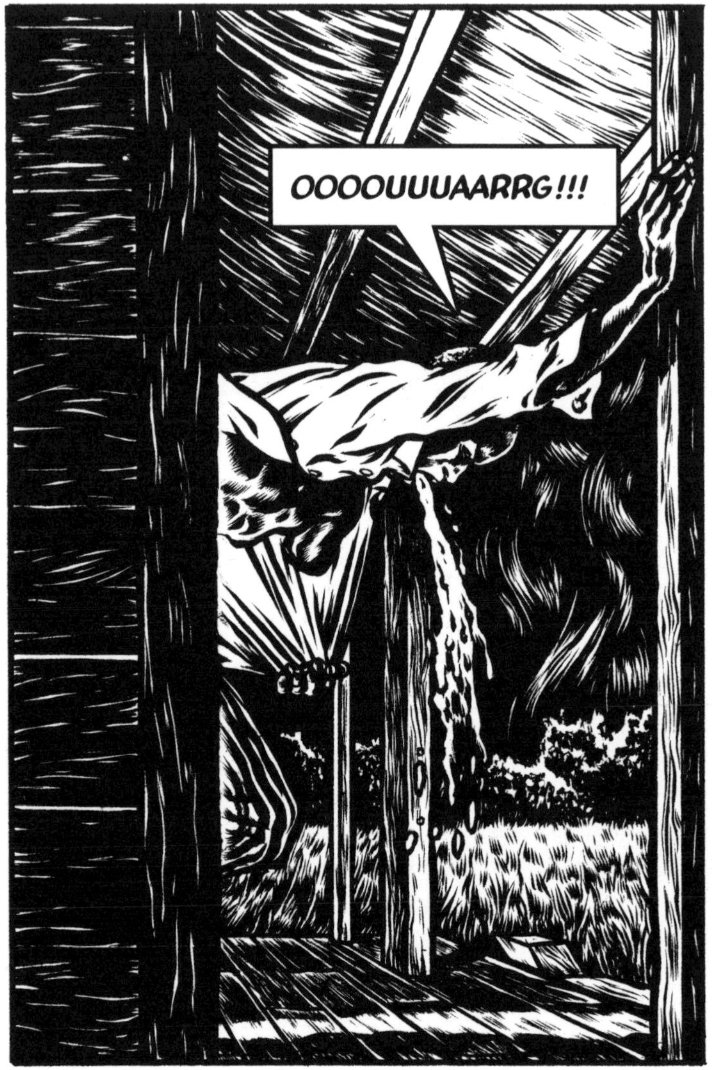
OOOOUUUAARRG!!!

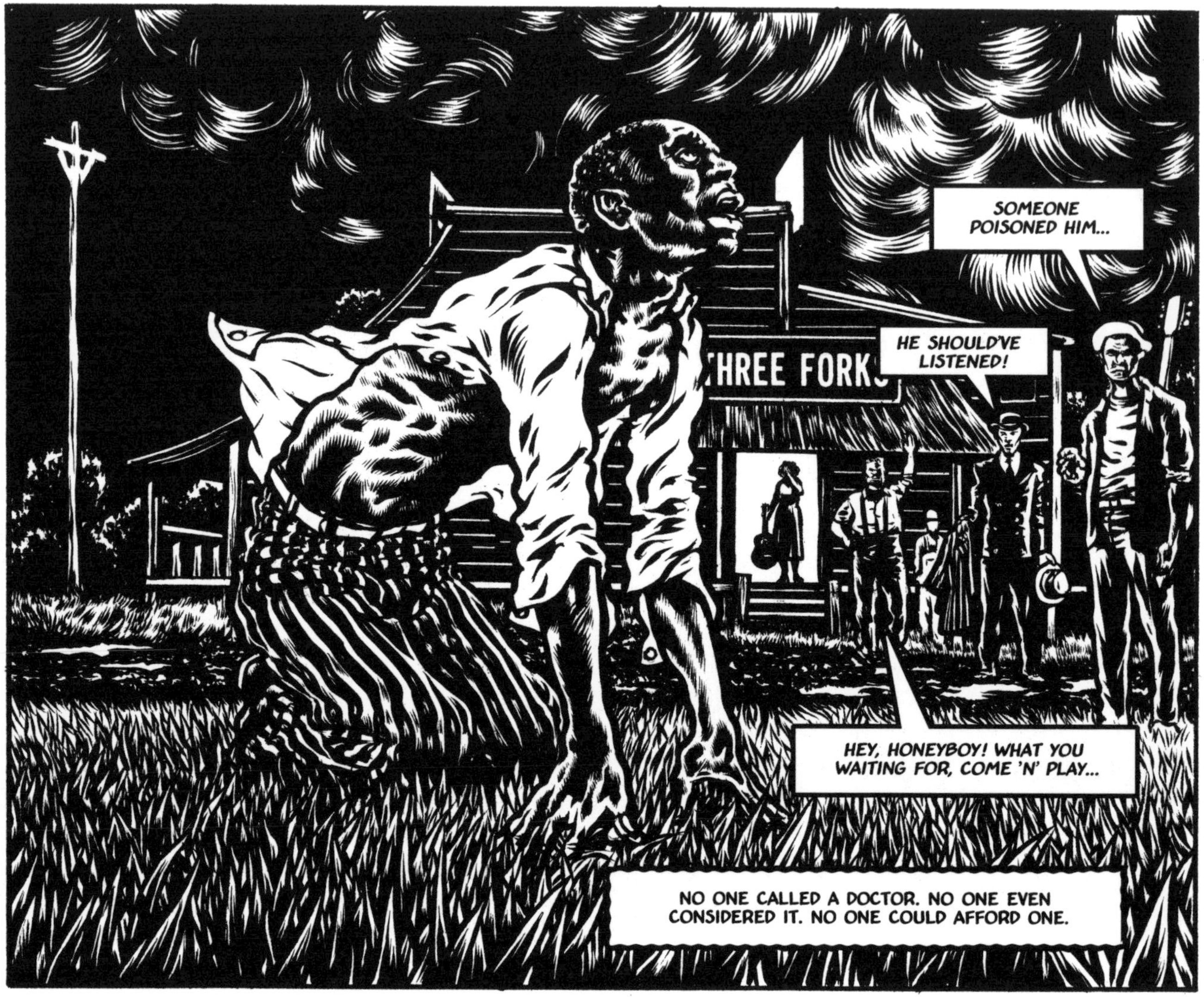
THREE FORKS
SOMEONE POISONED HIM...
HE SHOULD'VE LISTENED!
HEY, HONEYBOY! WHAT YOU WAITING FOR, COME 'N' PLAY...
NO ONE CALLED A DOCTOR. NO ONE EVEN CONSIDERED IT. NO ONE COULD AFFORD ONE.

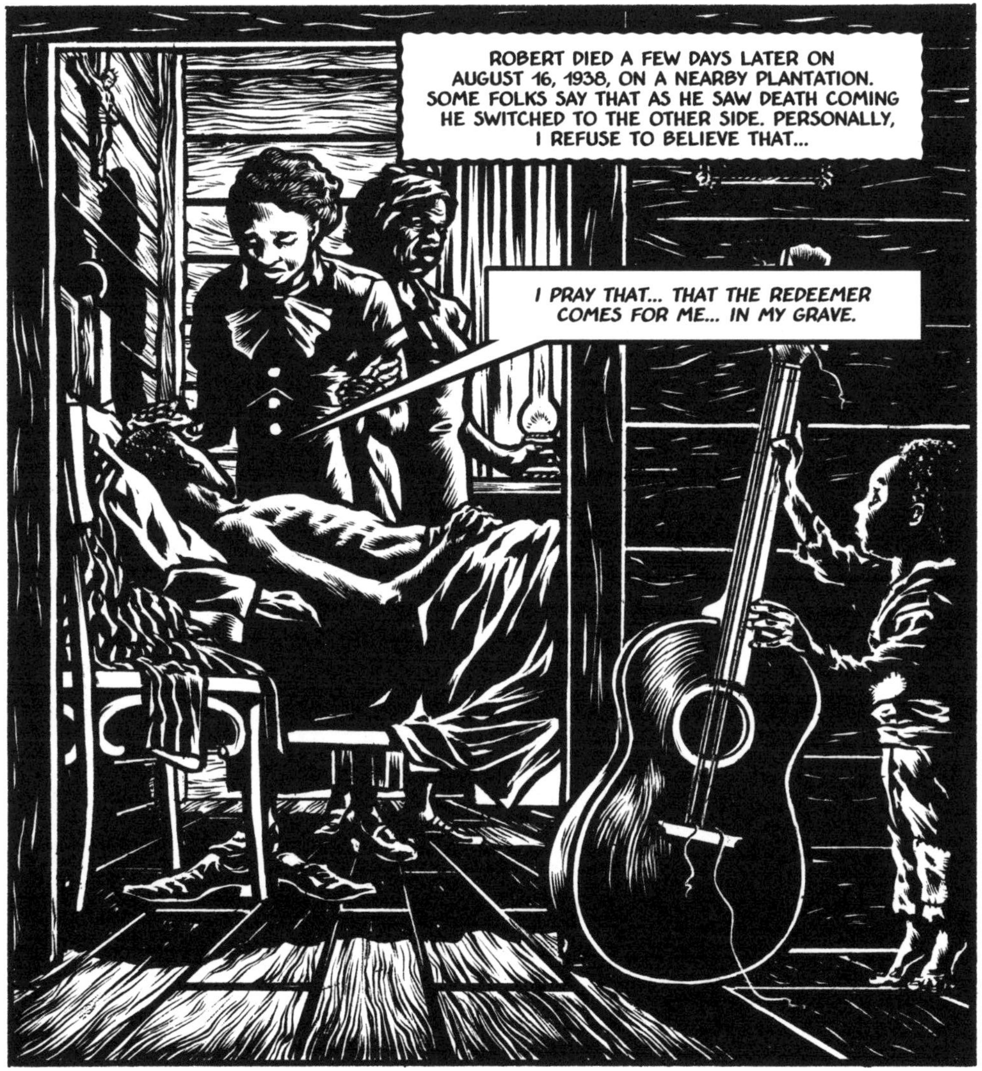
ROBERT DIED A FEW DAYS LATER ON AUGUST 16, 1938, ON A NEARBY PLANTATION. SOME FOLKS SAY THAT AS HE SAW DEATH COMING HE SWITCHED TO THE OTHER SIDE. PERSONALLY, I REFUSE TO BELIEVE THAT...
I PRAY THAT... THAT THE REDEEMER COMES FOR ME... IN MY GRAVE.

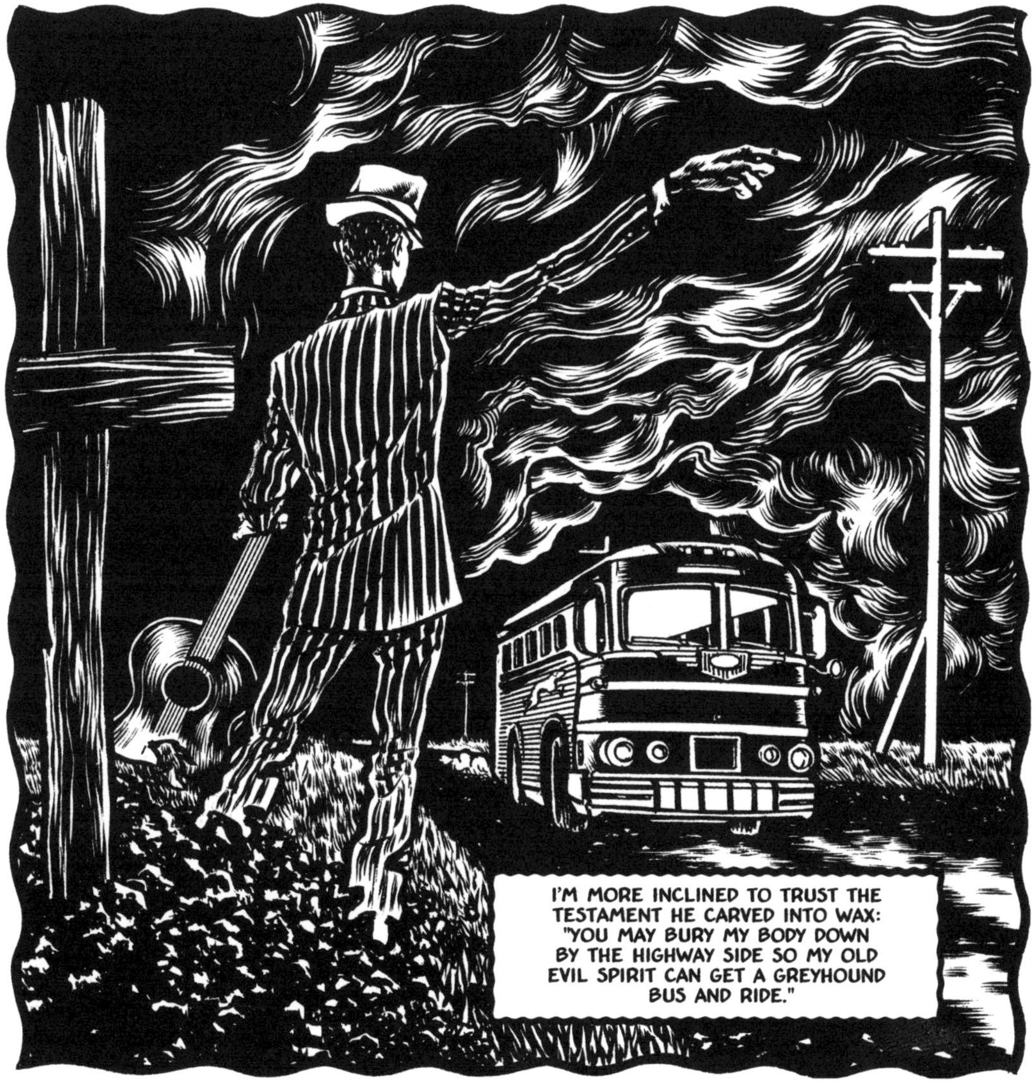
I'M MORE INCLINED TO TRUST THE TESTAMENT HE CARVED INTO WAX: "YOU MAY BURY MY BODY DOWN BY THE HIGHWAY SIDE SO MY OLD EVIL SPIRIT CAN GET A GREYHOUND BUS AND RIDE."

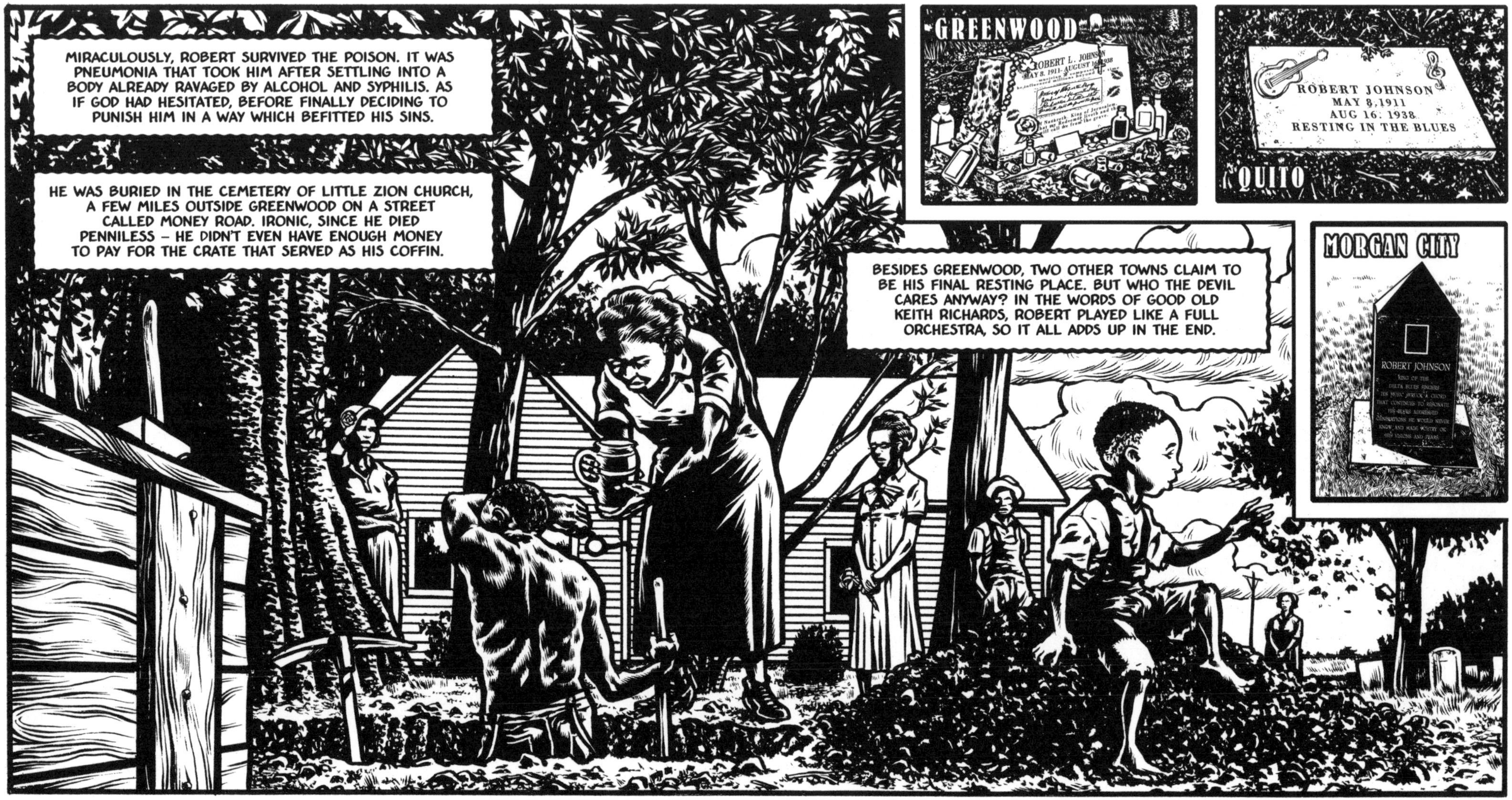

MIRACULOUSLY, ROBERT SURVIVED THE POISON. IT WAS PNEUMONIA THAT TOOK HIM AFTER SETTLING INTO A BODY ALREADY RAVAGED BY ALCOHOL AND SYPHILIS. AS IF GOD HAD HESITATED, BEFORE FINALLY DECIDING TO PUNISH HIM IN A WAY WHICH BEFITTED HIS SINS.
HE WAS BURIED IN THE CEMETERY OF LITTLE ZION CHURCH, A FEW MILES OUTSIDE GREENWOOD ON A STREET CALLED MONEY ROAD. IRONIC, SINCE HE DIED PENNILESS – HE DIDN'T EVEN HAVE ENOUGH MONEY TO PAY FOR THE CRATE THAT SERVED AS HIS COFFIN.
GREENWOOD
ROBERT L. JOHNSON
ROBERT JOHNSON
MAY 8,1911
AUG 16, 1938
RESTING IN THE BLUES
QUITO
MORGAN CITY
ROBERT JOHNSON
BESIDES GREENWOOD, TWO OTHER TOWNS CLAIM TO BE HIS FINAL RESTING PLACE. BUT WHO THE DEVIL CARES ANYWAY? IN THE WORDS OF GOOD OLD KEITH RICHARDS, ROBERT PLAYED LIKE A FULL ORCHESTRA, SO IT ALL ADDS UP IN THE END.

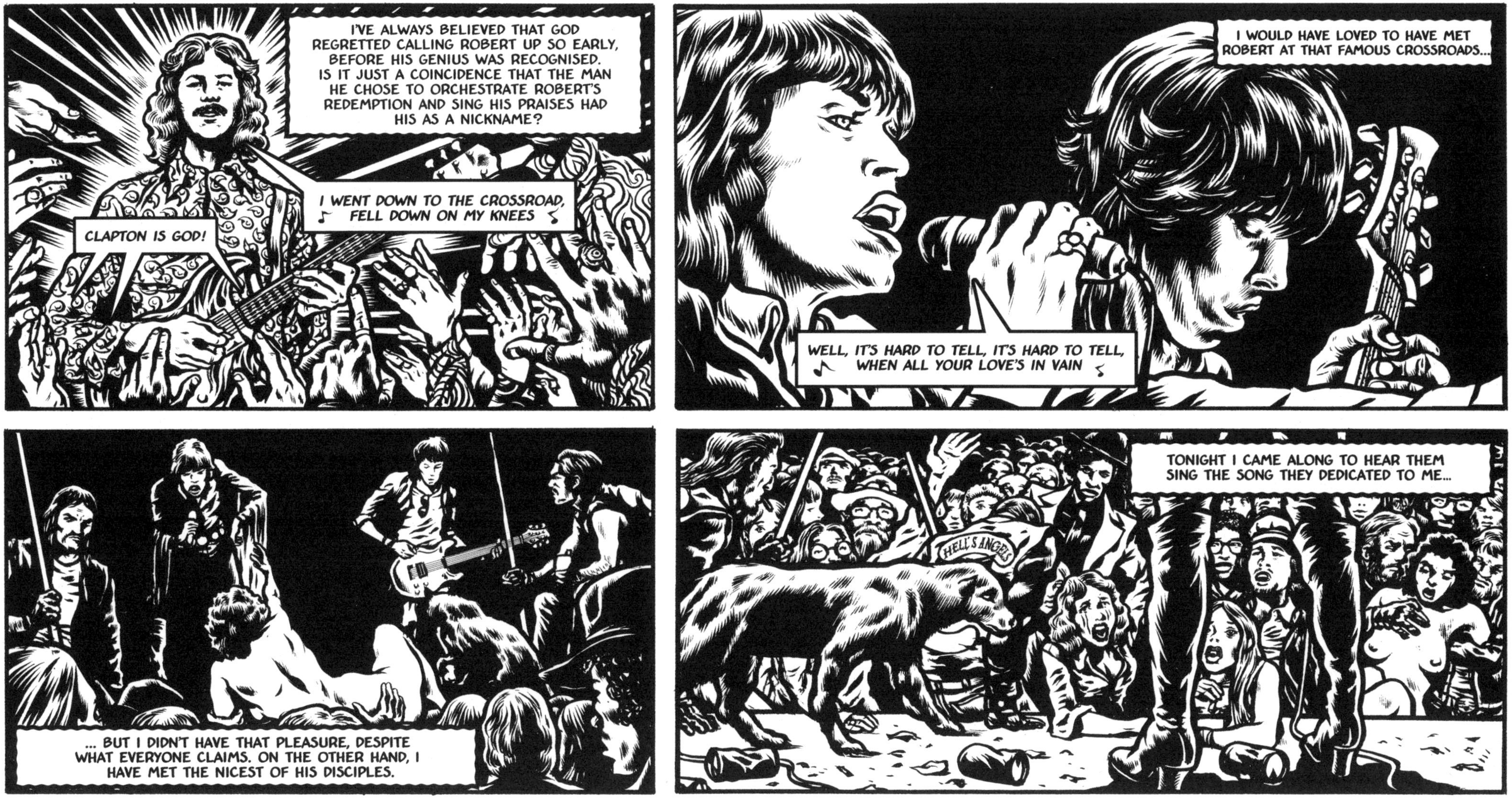
I'VE ALWAYS BELIEVED THAT GOD REGRETTED CALLING ROBERT UP SO EARLY, BEFORE HIS GENIUS WAS RECOGNISED. IS IT JUST A COINCIDENCE THAT THE MAN HE CHOSE TO ORCHESTRATE ROBERT'S REDEMPTION AND SING HIS PRAISES HAD HIS AS A NICKNAME?
I WENT DOWN TO THE CROSSROAD, FELL DOWN ON MY KNEES
CLAPTON IS GOD!
I WOULD HAVE LOVED TO HAVE MET ROBERT AT THAT FAMOUS CROSSROADS...
WELL, IT'S HARD TO TELL, IT'S HARD TO TELL, WHEN ALL YOUR LOVE'S IN VAIN
... BUT I DIDN'T HAVE THAT PLEASURE, DESPITE WHAT EVERYONE CLAIMS. ON THE OTHER HAND, I HAVE MET THE NICEST OF HIS DISCIPLES.
HELL'S ANGELS
TONIGHT I CAME ALONG TO HEAR THEM SING THE SONG THEY DEDICATED TO ME...

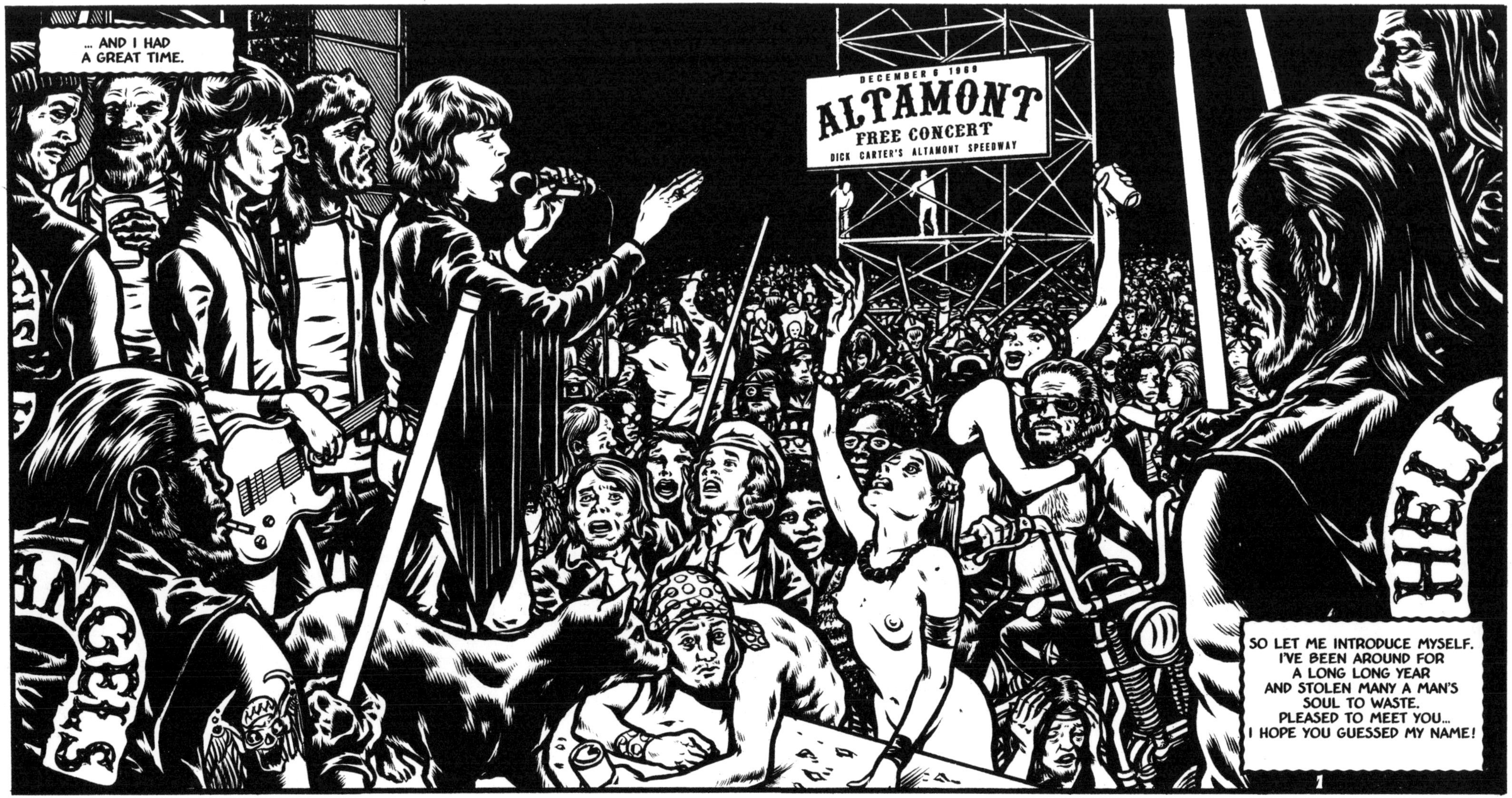
... AND I HAD
A GREAT TIME.
DECEMBER 6 1969
ALTAMONT
FREE CONCERT
DICK CARTER'S ALTAMONT SPEEDWAY
SO LET ME INTRODUCE MYSELF.
I'VE BEEN AROUND FOR
A LONG LONG YEAR
AND STOLEN MANY A MAN'S
SOUL TO WASTE.
PLEASED TO MEET YOU...
I HOPE YOU GUESSED MY NAME!

SONG BOOK

SONGS WRITTEN AND COMPOSED BY ROBERT JOHNSON

COME ON IN MY KITCHEN

You better come on in my kitchen
Babe, it's goin' to be rainin' outdoors

The woman I love, took from my best friend
Some joker got lucky, stole her back again
You better come on in my kitchen
Babe, it's goin' to be rainin' outdoors

Oh, she's gone, I know she won't come back
I've taken the last nickel out of her nation sack
You better come on in my kitchen
Baby, it's goin' to be rainin' outdoors

Oh, can't you hear that wind howl?
Oh, can't you hear that wind howl?
You better come on in my kitchen
Baby, it's goin' to be rainin' outdoors

When a woman gets in trouble, everybody throws her down
Lookin' for her good friend, none can't be found
You better come on in my kitchen
Baby, it's goin' to be rainin' outdoors

Winter time's comin', it's goin' to be slow
You can make the winter, babe, that's dry long so
You better come on in my kitchen
'Cause it's goin' to be rainin' outdoors

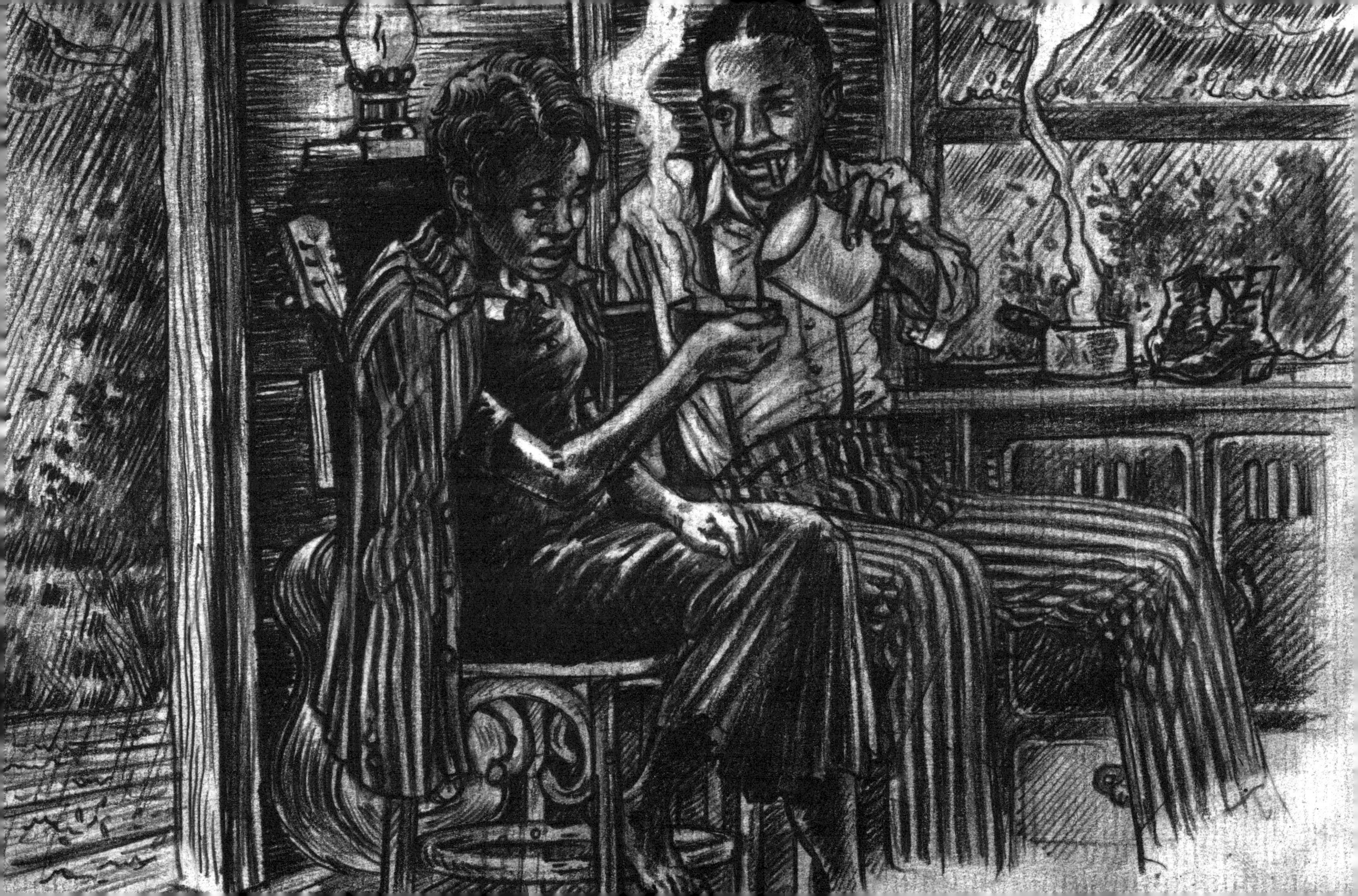

TERRAPLANE BLUES

And I feel so lonesome you hear me when I moan
And I feel so lonesome you hear me when I moan
Who been drivin' my Terraplane for years since I been gone ?

I said I flash your lights mama your horn won't even blow
Somebody's been running my batteries down here you see
I even flash my lights mama this horn won't even blow
Got a short in this connection hoo well way down below

I'm gon' hoist your hood mama I'm bound to check your oil
I'm gon' hoist your hood mama I'm bound to check your oil
I got a woman that I'm lovin' way down in Arkansas

Now you know the coils ain't even burnin'
Little generator won't get that spark
All's in a bad condition you gotta have these batteries charged and I'm cryin'
Please please don't do me wrong
Who been drivin' my Terraplane for years since I been gone ?

Mr. Highway man please don't block the road
Please please don't block the road
'Cause she's registrin' a cold one hundred
And I'm booked and I got to go

You you hear me weep and moan
Who been drivin' my Terraplane now for years since I been gone ?
I'm gon' get deep down in this connection keep on tanglin' with yo' wires
I'm gon' get deep down in this connection keep on tanglin' with yo' wires
And when I mash down on your little starter
Then your spark plug will give me fire

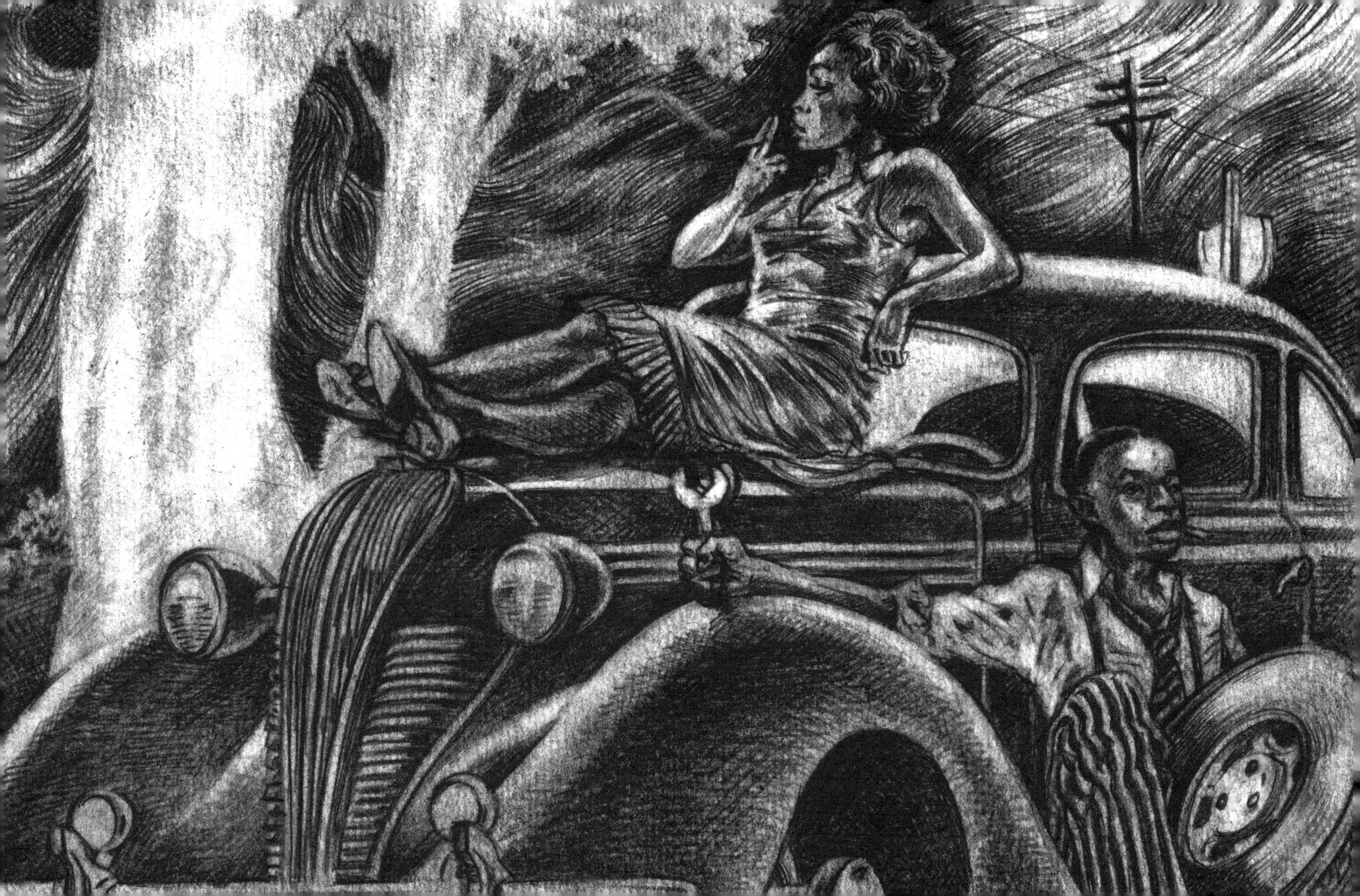

CROSS ROAD BLUES

I went to the crossroad, fell down on my knees
I went to the crossroad, fell down on my knees
Asked the Lord above: "Have mercy now, save poor Bob if you please"

Standin' at the crossroad, tried to flag a ride,
Ououh, yeeeeh, I tried to flag a ride
Ain't nobody seem to know me babe, everybody pass me by

Standin' at the crossroad baby, risin' sun, goin' down
Standin' at the crossroad baby, risin' sun goin' down
I believe to my soul now, poor Bob is sinkin' down

You can run, you can run, tell my friend Willie Brown
You can run, you can run, tell my friend Willie Brown
That I got the crossroad blues this mornin' Lord, babe I'm sinkin' down

And I went to the crossroad mama, I looked east and west
I went to the crossroad baby, I looked east and west
Lord I didn't have no sweet woman, well babe in my distress

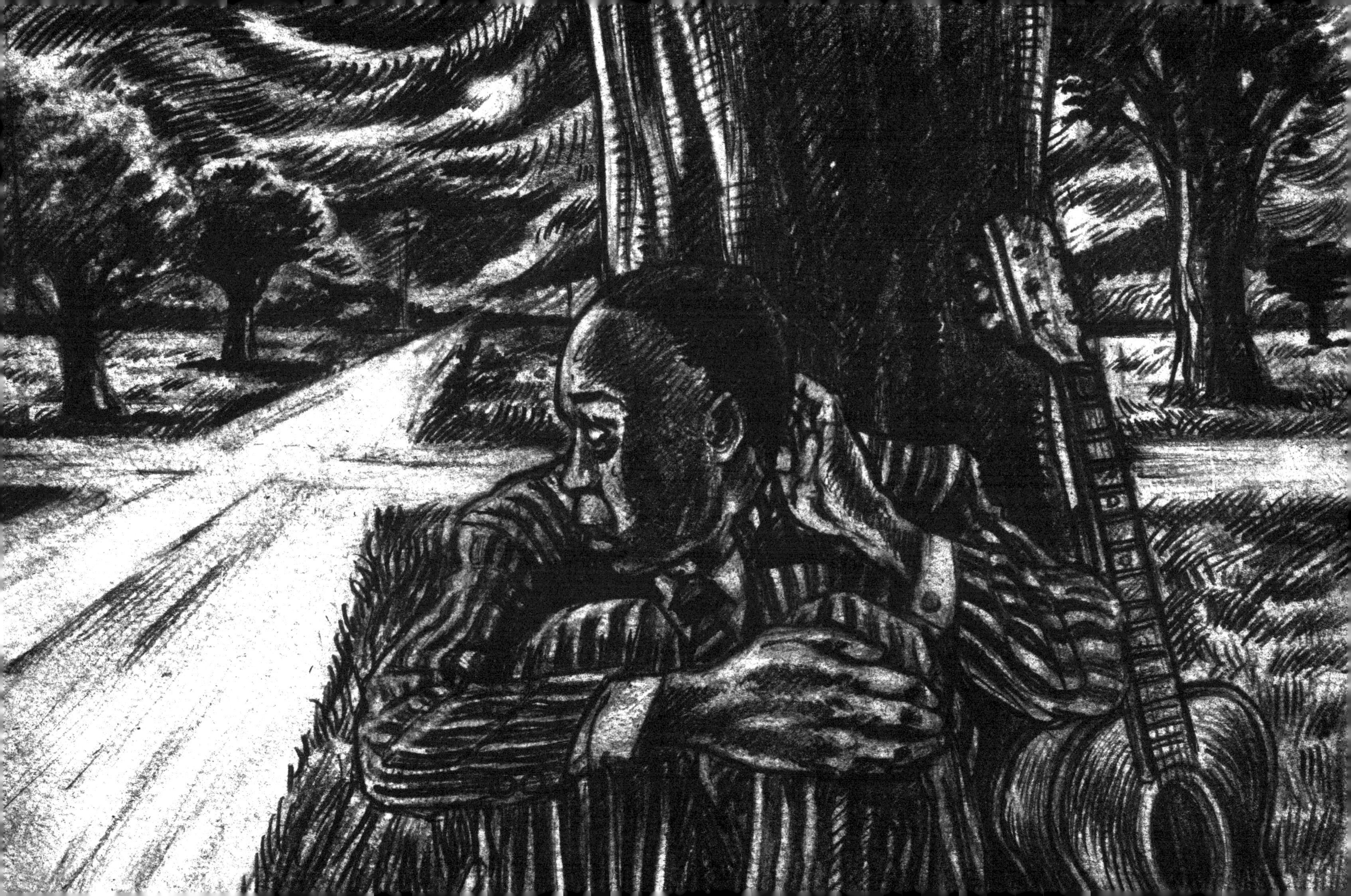

ME AND THE DEVIL BLUES

Early this mornin'
When you knocked upon my door
Early this mornin'
Ooh, when you knocked upon my door
And I said
"Hello, Satan, I believe it's time to go"

Me and the devil
Was walkin' side by side
Me and the devil
Ooh, was walkin' side by side
I'm goin' to beat my woman
Until I get satisfied

She say, "You don't see why
That I will dog 'round"
She say, "You don't see why
Ooh, that I be dog 'round"
It must be that old evil spirit
So deep down in the ground

You may bury my body
Down by the highway side
You may bury my body
Ooh, down by the highway side
So my old evil spirit
Can get a Greyhound bus and ride

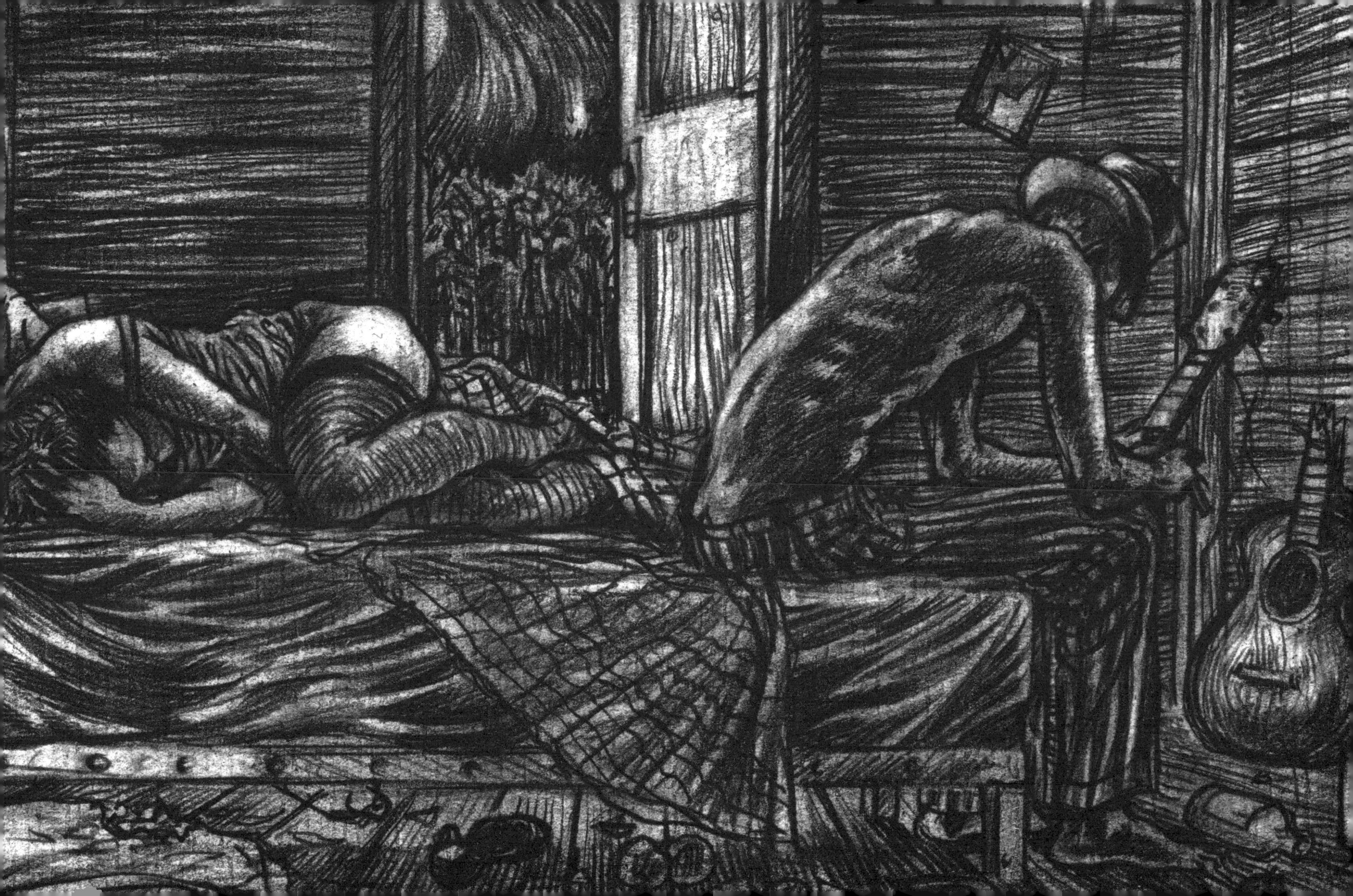

LOVE IN VAIN

And I followed her to the station with her suitcase in my hand
And I followed her to the station with her suitcase in my hand
Well it's hard to tell, it's hard to tell, when all your love's in vain
All my love's in vain

When the train rolled up to the station, I looked her in the eye
When the train rolled up to the station, and I looked her in the eye
Well I was lonesome I felt so lonesome, and I could not help but cry
All my love's in vain

The train it left the station, was two lights on behind
When the train it left the station, was two lights on behind
Well the blue light was my blues and the red light was my mind
All my love's in vain

Ooh Willie Mae
Ooh Willie Mae
All my love's in vain

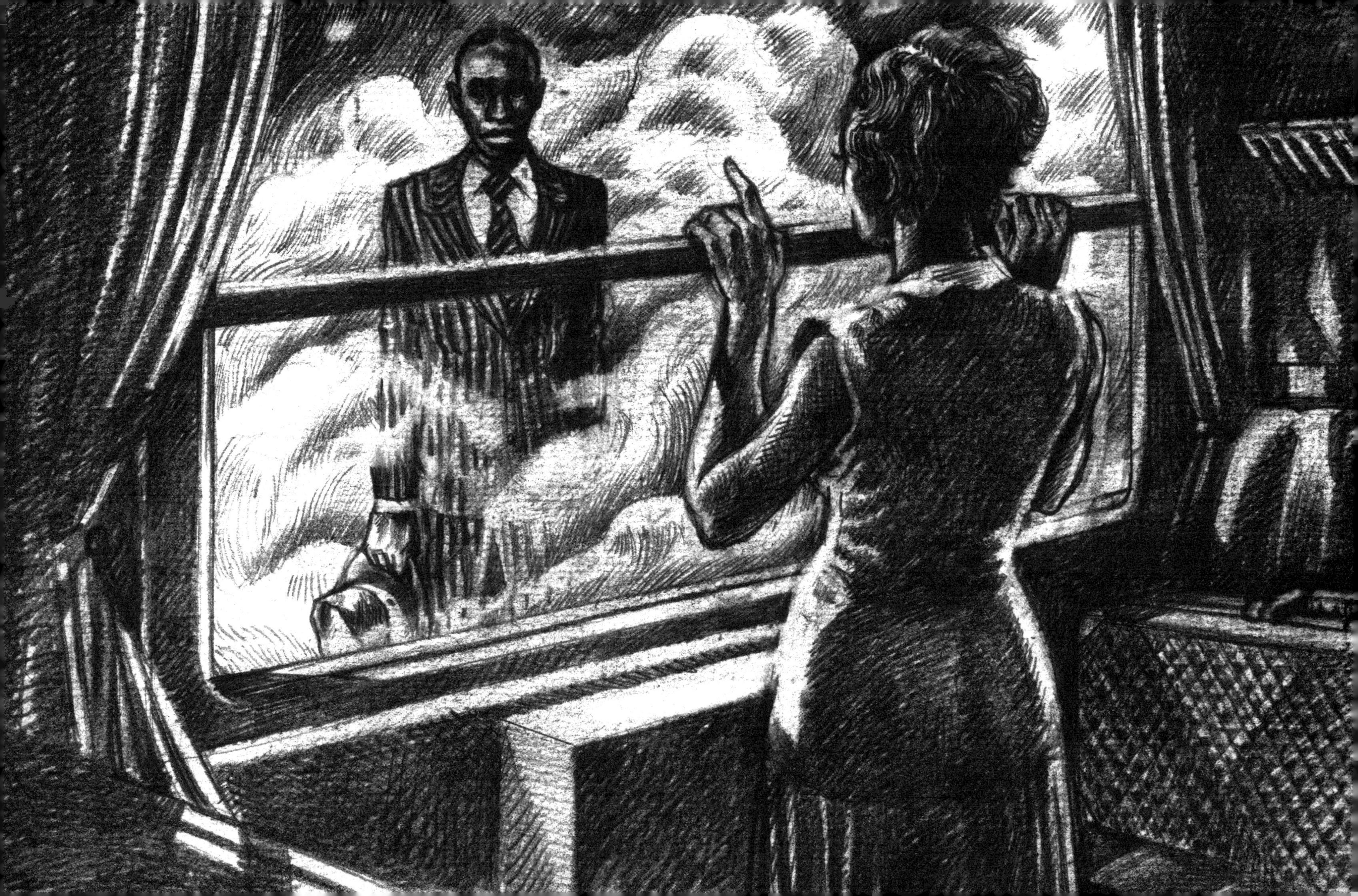

SWEET HOME CHICAGO

Oh, baby don't you want to go ?
Oh, baby don't you want to go ?
Back to the land of California
To my sweet home Chicago

Oh, baby don't you want to go ?
Oh, baby don't you want to go ?
Back to the land of California
To my sweet home Chicago

Now one and one is two
Two and two is four
I'm heavy loaded baby
I'm booked, I gotta go

Cryin', baby
Honey, don't you want to go ?
Back to the land of California
To my sweet home Chicago

Now two and two is four
Four and two is six
You gonna keep monkeyin' 'round, here friend-boy
You gonna get your business all in a trick

But I'm cryin' baby
Honey, don't you wanna go ?
Back to the land of California
To my sweet home Chicago

Now six and two is eight
Eight and two is ten
Friend-boy she trick you one time
She sure gonna do it again

But I'm cryin' hey
Baby don't you want to go ?
To the land of California
To my sweet home Chicago

I'm goin' to California
From there to Des Moines, Iowa
Somebody will tell me that you
Need my help someday

Cryin', hey hey
Baby don't you want to go ?
Back to the land of California
To my sweet home Chicago

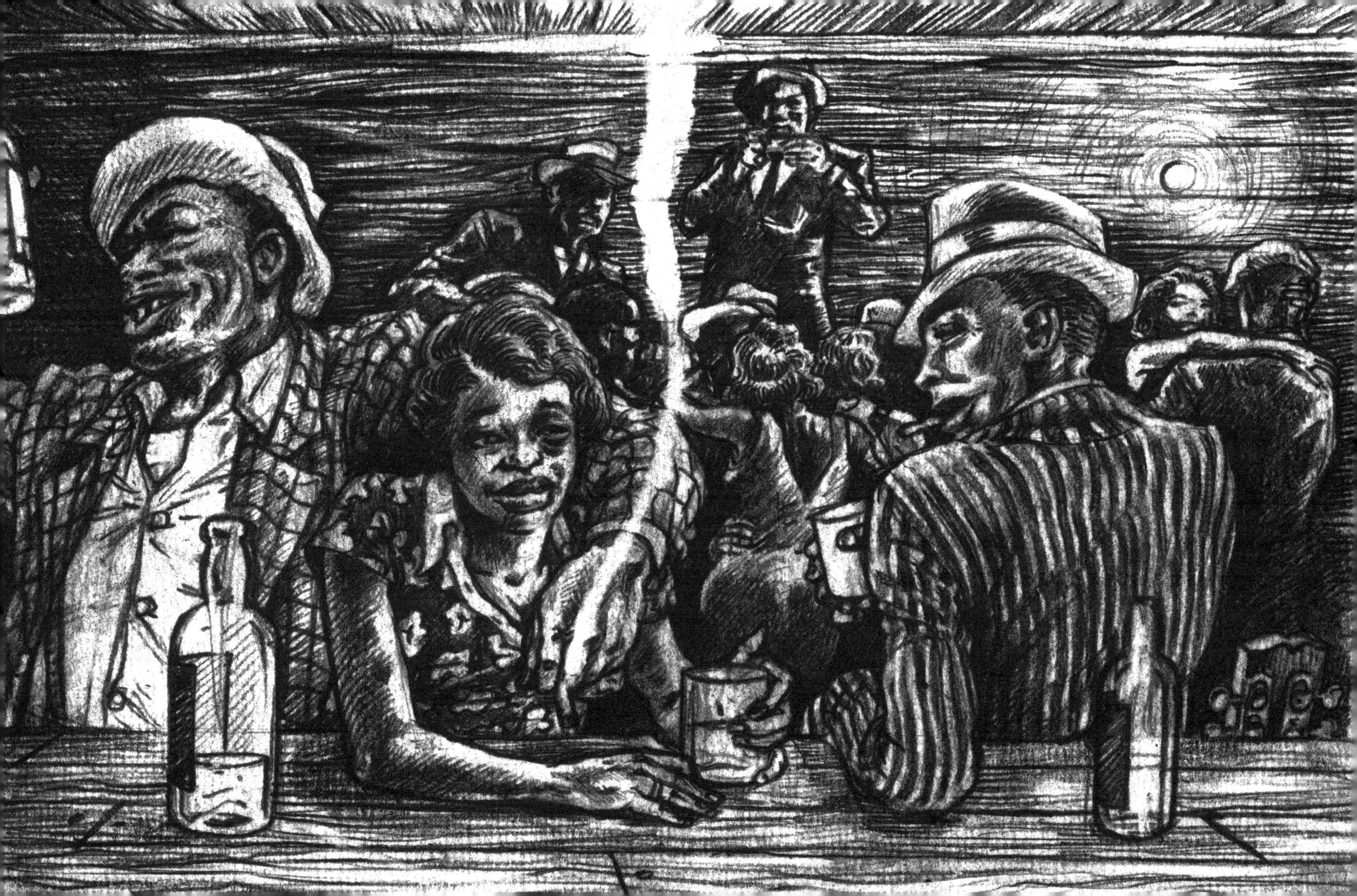

32-20 BLUES

I send for my baby and she don't come
I send for my baby, man, and she don't come
All the doctors in Hot Springs, they sure can't help her none

And if she gets unruly, things she don't wanna do
And if she gets unruly and thinks she don't wanna do
Take my 32-20, now, and cut her half in two

She got a 38 special but I believe it's most too light
She got a 38 special but I believe it's most too light
I got a 32-20, got to make the camps alright

I send for my baby, man, and she don't come
I send for my baby, man, and she don't come
All the doctors in Hot Springs sure can't help her none

I'm gonna shoot my pistol, I'm gonna shoot my Gatling gun
I'm gonna shoot my pistol, gotta shoot my Gatling gun
You made me love you, now your man have come

Baby, where'd you stay last night ?
Baby, where'd you stay last night ?
You got your hair all tangled and you ain't talkin' right

38 special, boys, do it very well
38 special, boys, it do very well
I got a 32-20 now and it's a burnin'

If I send for my baby, man, and she don't come
If I send for my baby, man, and she don't come
All the doctors in Wisconsin sure can't help her none

Hey, hey baby, where'd you stay last night ?
Hey, hey baby, where'd you stay last night ?
You didn't come home until the sun was shining bright

Ah boy, I just can't take my rest
Ah boy, I just can't take my rest
With this 32-20 laying up and down my breast

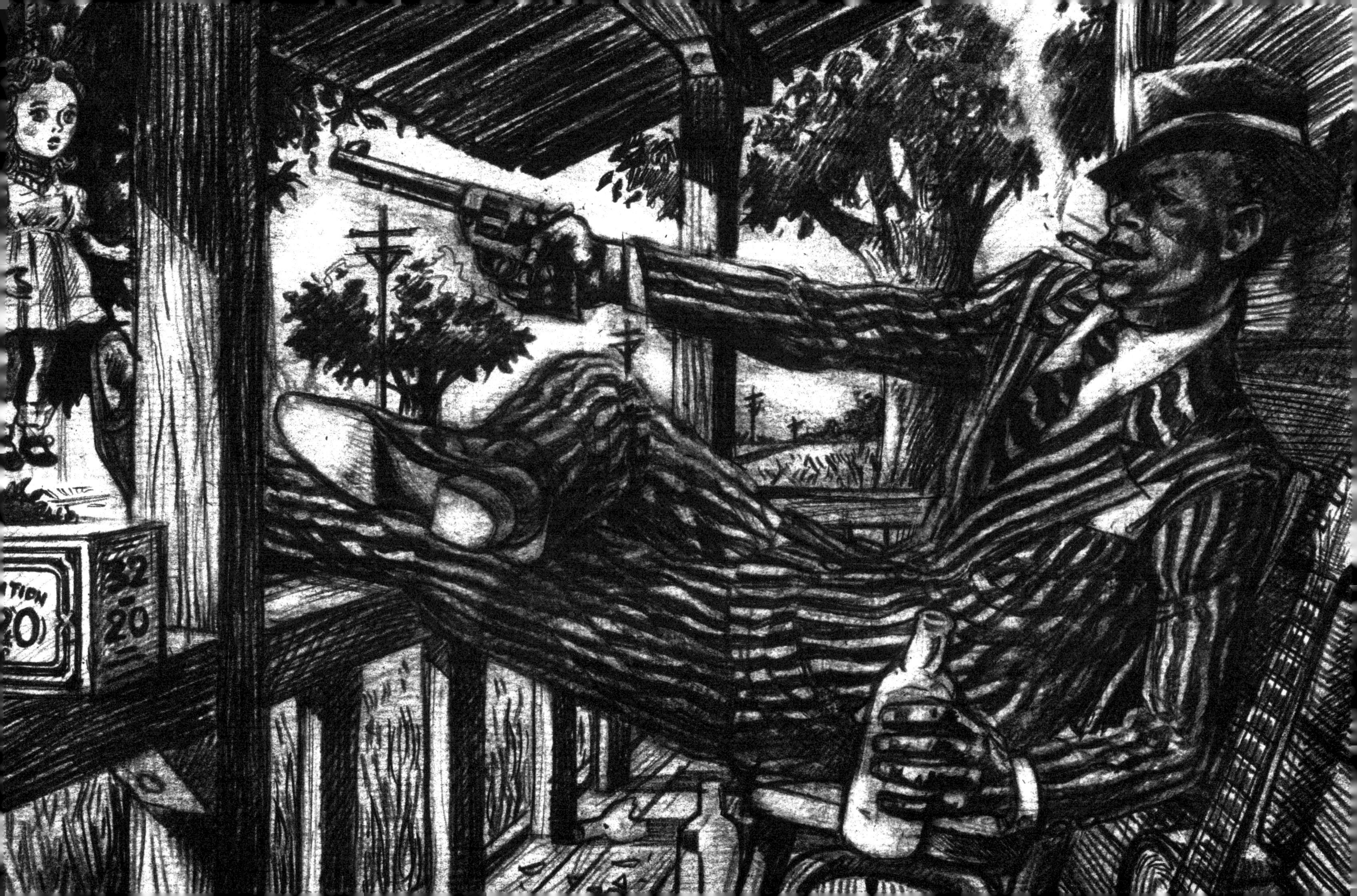
TION
20
32-20

BIBLIOGRAPHY

ROBERT JOHNSON

Robert Johnson, Samuel B. Charters (New York: Oak Publications), 1972

Robert Johnson, The Complete Recordings, livret du CD, Steve LaVere (Columbia), 1990

À la recherche de Robert Johnson, Peter Guralnick (Castor Music), 1998

Mystery Train: Images de l'Amérique à travers le Rock'n'roll, Greil Marcus (Allia), 2001

Robert Johnson Lost and Found, Barry Lee Pearson et Bill Mc Culloch (University of Illinois Press), 2003

Escaping the Delta, Robert Johnson and the Invention of Blues, Elijah Wald (Amistad), 2004

Robert Johnson, Mythmaking and Contemporary American Culture, Patricia R. Shroeder (University of Illinois Press), 2004

Crossroads, The Life and Afterlife of Blues Legend Robert Johnson, Tom Graves (Rythm Oil Publications), 2008

Les Enfers du Rock, Philippe Manœuvre (Tana), 2009

BLUES

The Country Blues, Samuel B. Charters (Da Capo Press), 1959

Le Monde du Blues, Paul Oliver (10-18), 1962

Le Peuple du Blues, LeRoi Jones (Folio, Gallimard), 1963

Blues from the Delta, William R. Ferris (Da Capo Press), 1970

Feel Like Going Home, Légendes du Blues et pionniers du Rock'n'Roll, Peter Guralnick (Rivages Rouges), 1971

Devil's Music, Une Histoire du Blues, Giles Oakley (Denoël), 1976

Le Blues, Gérard Herzhaft (Puf, Que sais-je ?), 1981

Deep Blues, Robert Palmer (Penguin), 1982

Talkin' that Talk, Le Langage du Blues et du Jazz, Jean-Paul Levet (Hatier), 1992

Nothing but the Blues, Lawrence Cohn (Abbeville Press), 1993

Le Pays où naquit le Blues, Alan Lomax (Les Fondeurs de Briques), 1993

La Grande Encyclopédie du Blues, Gérard Herzhaft (Fayard), 1997

Chasin' that Devil Music: Searchin' for the Blues, Gayle Dean Wardlow (Backbeat Books), 1998

Blackface, Nick Tosches (Allia), 2001

Martin Scorsese présente : Le Blues, Peter Guralnick, Robert Santelli, Holly George-Warren et Christopher John Farley (Naïve), 2003

Memphis Blues, Jean-Jacques Milteau et Sebastian Danchin (Éditions du Chêne), 2005

The Language of the Blues, From Alcorub to Zuzu, Debra Devi (True Nature Books), 2006

Héros du Blues, du Jazz et de la Country, Robert Crumb, Stephen Calt, David Jasen et Richard Nevins (Éditions de la Martinière), 2008

Delta Blues, Ted Gioa (W. W. Norton), 2008

Blues Traveling, The Holy Sites of Delta Blues, Steve Cheseborough (University Press of Mississipi), 2009

Blues, Alain Gerber (Fayard), 2009

The Blues. A Very Short Introduction, Elijah Wald (Oxford University Press), 2010

Hidden History of Mississippi Blues, Roger Stolle (The History Press), 2011

Philosophie du Blues. Une éthique de l'errance solitaire, Philippe Paraire (Les Éditions de l'Épervier), 2012

VOODOO

Le Vaudou haïtien, Alfred Métraux (Gallimard), 1958

Le Vaudou, Charles Planson (Ma Éditions), 1987

FILMOGRAPHY

Mississippi Blues, Bertrand Tavernier et Robert Parrish , 1988

Deep Blues: A Musical Pilgrimage to the Crossroads, Robert Mugge, 1990

The Search for Robert Johnson, Chris Hunt, 1992

Can't You Hear the Wind Howl ? The Life & Music of Robert Johnson, Peter W. Meyer, 1997

Stop Breaking Down, Glenn Marzano, 1999

Devil's Fire, Charles Burnett, 2006

WEBOGRAPHY

Robert Johnson Blues Foundation : robertjohnsonbluesfoundation.org

Mississippi Blues Trail : msbluestrail.org

The Delta Blues : tdblues.com

ACKNOWLEDGEMENTS

Lawrence Cohn for his enthusiasm and encouragement.

Samuel B. Charters, Mack McCormick, Peter Guralnick, Robert Palmer,
Steve LaVere, Elijah Wald, Gérard Herzhaft and all the experts on the blues
whose work has been of invaluable assistance.

Dorothea Lange and Walker Evans for their photos from
the 1930s, which have been equally invaluable.

Tom Wilson, whose illustration for the album sleeve of
Robert Johnson – King of the Delta Blues Singers Vol. 2 (Columbia)
is evoked by Mezzo on page 36 of this book.

Robert Crumb, an inexhaustible source of admiration and inspiration.

Sylvester Hoover for his company on an unforgettable walk
in Greenwood, Mississippi.

The Robert Johnson Blues Foundation for their warm welcome
at Crystal Springs, Mississippi.

Nicolas Finet for his good-humoured and knowledgeable support.

Judith Harris for her expert proofreading.

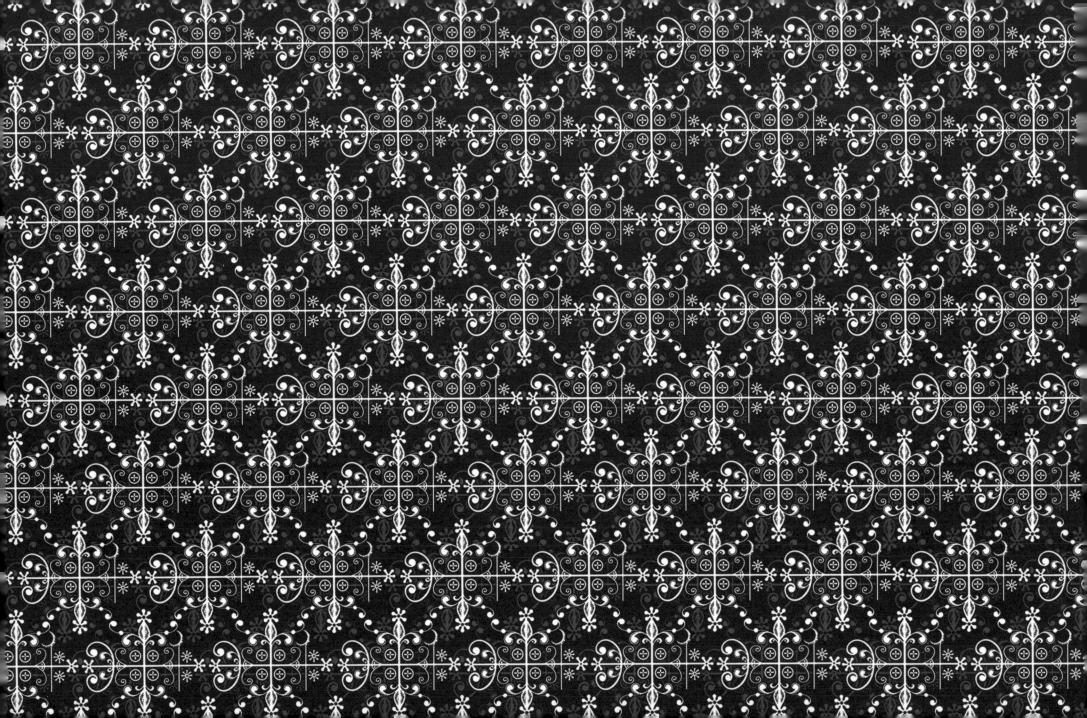